YOU CAN MAKE A DIFFERENCE!

YOU CAN MAKE A DIFFERENCE!

A Creative Workbook and Journal for Young Activists

Sherry Paris

Illustrated by Sherry Paris

Jessica Kingsley Publishers
London and Philadelphia

First published in Great Britain in 2022 by Jessica Kingsley Publishers
An Hachette Company

1

Copyright © Sherry Paris 2022
Illustrations copyright © Sherry Paris 2022

The information contained in this book is not intended to replace the
services of trained medical professionals or to be a substitute for medical
advice. You are advised to consult a doctor on any matters relating to
your health and mental health, and in particular on any matters that may
require diagnosis or medical attention.

A CIP catalogue record for this title is available from the British Library
and the Library of Congress

ISBN 978 1 78775 648 9
eISBN 978 1 78775 649 6

Printed and bound in the United States by Integrated Books International

Jessica Kingsley Publishers' policy is to use papers that are natural,
renewable and recyclable products and made from wood grown
in sustainable forests. The logging and manufacturing processes
are expected to conform to the environmental regulations
of the country of origin.

Jessica Kingsley Publishers
Carmelite House
50 Victoria Embankment
London EC4Y 0DZ

www.jkp.com

DEDICATIONS & GRATITUDE

To Mel Tirado, beloved spouse, for abundant support and devotion. Infinite love and gratitude.

To David Paris, beloved father, for enthusiastic encouragement to write this book (for at least a decade!).

To Elaine Paris, beloved mother, for timeless creativity and inspiration.

To Jessica Kingsley Publishers for creating books that truly make a difference. May this book contribute to that purpose. Sincere appreciation to Andrew James, Editorial Director, and the whole team at JKP.

To Alise Mackey, Grayson Ray, Helen Everbach and Soul Cooke for sharing stories and consulting time throughout the writing and editing process. Deep gratitude for your support and friendship.

To all Diversity Trainers for your dedication to making a difference. Heartfelt gratitude for courageously creating change through education.

To family and friends for devoted care, laughter and love. Enduring gratitude to Aditi Oakley, staunch supporter!

To the ancestors, all respect and love. May this book offering please you and make you proud. Kinehora.

To all the people and communities who devote their energies to creating a more just world for the greater good. To those who exist(ed) and persist(ed) through oppressive systems, to those who resist(ed), to those who survive(d) and thrive(d), and to those who did/do/may not. Honoring your names, memories and legacies, especially the Lenape, who are currently and have been for thousands of years, the inhabitants and stewards of Lenapehoking, including the land currently referred to as Philadelphia, where this book emerged.

CONTENTS

INTRODUCTION

Welcome! Thank you for your care and concern for humanity and the world. That motivation will serve you well in life. I am delighted that you are on this journey towards a greater understanding of yourself and others, towards taking action on behalf of yourself and others, and towards creating a better version of society. Your efforts are so important. You've got this!

This book is a resource for people, especially young people, who want to make a difference. Social justice skills and action are essential and urgently needed now. Together, let's explore intersecting identities and be conscious of the systems underpinning injustice to help turn our concerns into positive action. Seeing a bigger picture often helps us understand ourselves and others. How can we be thoughtful and connect across diverse identities and communities to others who have different life experiences than we do to create change?

What is social justice?

Social justice is an umbrella term for a set of movements, such as racial justice and disability justice, intended to create a more equitable society. Where does social justice happen? Everywhere! Anywhere people are taking action to remedy instances of prejudice and discrimination and dismantle systems of injustice. You and your action are key to resolving our current issues and creating different systems that will serve and support all people. You have the power to make change, to do things differently.

The way to create change

Are you trying to figure out how to make social change to correct injustice? Is there a best way? There are countless ways to make a difference. Every action that is taken to recognize the humanity in all people with liberation and justice in mind contributes to disrupting and dismantling systems of oppression. There are many ways systems of oppression can operate, so there must be multiple approaches to systemic change. Everyone has a part to play and can make a difference in little and big ways.

How do you feel about oppression? Check as many options as apply to you (✓):

❏   I can't take it anymore!

❏   This system has got to go!

❏   I object!

❏   It breaks my heart

❏   I refuse to participate

❏   I will not allow this to continue

❏   I will not be complicit (part of the continued injustice)

❏   Write in: ....

Whether big or small, all actions towards social justice are needed. Actions at every level and in every capacity make a difference. We may know the impact of our efforts. We may not. What does it mean to cultivate connections with people, to dismantle our social conditioning and the systems which perpetuate injustice, to help alleviate suffering and work towards justice?

You can begin from where you are right now. Throughout the book there are questions and activities designed to help you get to know yourself better, including paying attention to your mind and body. Our bodies are constantly sending us signals about how we experience the world. Do we notice those cues? Can we cultivate an awareness of our responses to our own thoughts, feelings and sensations? Let's develop a body-awareness practice! This will serve us through life as we encounter social messages and situations and work towards social justice. Do you already practice noticing how you feel in your body? Is this a new idea for you? Create space for self-awareness and reflection every day. Check in with yourself. Ask yourself, "How is my breathing in this moment?" and, "How is my body experiencing this event/news?" How are thoughts, emotions and sensations resonating in your body? Pausing to experience how we feel may help us cultivate compassion for ourselves and others. Author, educator, artist and activist Sonya Renee Taylor says, "As we learn to make peace with our bodies and make peace with other people's bodies, we create an opening for creating a more just and equitable world."[1]

Committed to making the world a better place?

Maybe you think the world is already a perfectly wonderful place. Maybe you think the world is beyond saving. Maybe you think that you are just one person and question your potential impact. You never know who you will help (including yourself!). Stay encouraged! Your energies are needed. Your efforts make a difference!

Thank you for letting me be your companion on this journey of self-discovery and empowerment. I recognize your strength and power.

Seeds to plant and grow

These ideas are gems! Sit with them. Hold them. Let's consider them seeds to plant and grow throughout the book and in life. What seeds have you already planted? Put a check mark (✓) next to items you already practice. For seeds you are starting to plant now, place a star/asterisk (*) next to the description.

- ❏ Acceptance: Do you allow and encourage yourself and other people to be just as you/they are in all facets and aspects?

- ❏ Body awareness: Do you regularly notice what sensations or experiences are happening in your body?

❏   Commitment to ally action: Do you practice showing up, speaking up, challenging harmful systems and creating safe/brave and welcoming spaces for all? Who do you stand in solidarity with? How do you do that?

❏   Compassion: Do you cultivate care with a willingness to help? Can you have concern for yourself as you would for a friend or loved one? What does that look like, sound like, feel like?

❏   Consent: Do you have awareness of and respect for when you or someone else wants and agrees to do something?

❏   Cultural humility: Do you approach other cultures (and your own) with respect and genuine interest, and take time to learn?

❏   Empathy: Do you practice understanding and relating to other people's feelings (even if you have not had that exact experience or perspective)?

❏   Empowerment: Do you stand in your truth and recognize that you have the power to make a difference? Do you collaborate with others who are taking that approach?

❏   Healthy boundaries: Do you set limits on what you want and do not want, what you will or will not accept?

❏   Lifelong learning: Do you seek opportunities to grow and understand more?

❏   Love: Who do you love? How do you express your love and care for humans, animals, nature and the planet? Does love motivate you to work towards social justice?

❏   Mindfulness: Do you notice your thoughts and bodily sensations?

❏   Mutual support: Do you cultivate healthy relationships and connections to social groups which benefit all involved?

❏   Perspective-taking: Are you curious about what a thought, feeling, experience or situation looks like when viewed from another angle or another person's viewpoint? Do you take the time to understand others' perspectives?

❏ Self-advocacy: Do you practice letting your needs be known? For example, do you need to sit close to the teacher/professor or point of instruction in order to see, hear or focus? Do you need movement breaks or fidgeting to focus and promote calm? Accessible parking? Ramps and elevators? Language interpretation? Do you need to negotiate a menu to ensure your dietary needs are met? How and when do you communicate your needs?

❏ Self-care and self-love: Do you pay attention to what makes you feel more like yourself and in a better space? Do you notice what makes you feel drained, depleted or takes you out of yourself? Do you nurture yourself with opportunities to feel good/better? Do you accept and have compassion for yourself through all of your experiences?

Caring Crystals and Guiding Gems

What is a game changer?

Games are played according to rules. Similarly, there are expectations in the "game" of society. What are the rules, both spoken and unspoken? Who are the makers of the rules? Who enforces the rules? Which rules are taught explicitly and which are enforced through other methods? Who benefits from the rules? Who is less likely to benefit from the rules? Who is at a disadvantage from or is hindered by the rules? Do we need to play this game and by these rules?

You can be a game changer. Your willingness to recognize the game that is being played is transformative. Your decision to focus on justice and take action moves us as a society to a better place. Trust that the efforts that you make now create change immediately and going forward. Proclaim it: "I am a game changer!"

You are not alone. There are so many people who are with you and willing to make changes for the good of all. Think big. Envision a world in which everyone is included, everyone belongs, everyone's needs are met. Think that sounds overly ambitious? It is. **It must be.** Collectively, we must dream big to create the change that is needed. We will envision the world in which we want to live in Chapter 8. So exciting!

Humans are complex. We have a vast set of characteristics and identities. One identity cannot be separated from the others without making us a different person. We are often put into identity boxes for other people's convenience such as, "Oh, she's Muslim" or, "Oh, he's gay" or, "Oh, they are autistic," as if that one characteristic defines all of who we are. In any situation, one identity may be more prominent than other identities but we are more than just one aspect! And any given aspect has many different considerations and nuances to it. We may experience limitations imposed on us by social expectations or social barriers, but the truth is that we are beautifully multifaceted and so much more than just a compilation of characteristics. We are limitless! Let's tap into our unlimited potential together to figure out how to make this world work for all of us!

Activities

Throughout the book there are activities. These are just for you! If you would like to write in the book, please do so. If you prefer to keep a journal or notebook, go for that option! If you want to record your answers via voice or video or another method, do it. Make it work for you! You are invited to engage with the activities for fun and personal growth. It is not required that you complete all (or even any) of the activities. They are there to help you self-reflect and explore new ideas and revisit concepts that may already be near and dear to your heart. Please take time to color the illustrations throughout the book!

If you are using this book with a group, please allow for variety in individual engagement. If someone wants to dance their responses rather than saying them aloud or writing them down, allow it! If the group wants to change the activity to suit the needs of the members or to better align with the mission of the group, please adapt the directions! Make everything suit your group's needs. Be flexible. Let things evolve organically to be most inclusive.

Featured stories

I find joy, inspiration and connection in spaces where people are encouraged to be fully themselves, express themselves and witness each other. I love hearing stories of people who are making a difference. I am excited to offer you an opportunity to hear from four young people who are devoted to making a difference for social justice. They are game changers! They have graciously allowed me to interview them to bring their stories to you and they send you good wishes. Alise Mackey, Grayson Ray, Helen Everbach and Soul Cooke share their experiences of injustice, resilience, resistance, joy, empowerment, liberation and everyday action as well as some advice for people who want to make a difference. I hope you find affirmation and inspiration in their stories. As you read the interview responses, you will notice the conversational tone. Imagine you are sitting with friends. Experience the interviewees speaking directly to you. The responses in the book are excerpts from the full interviews.

I had the great honor of collaborating with the four featured interviewees when they were high school students (aged 14–18). I am happy to share that we have evolved our teacher–student relationships into friendships. Alise, Grayson, Helen and Soul are my heroes! They are my role models! Alise, Helen and Soul were leaders of a school-based diversity training project called Diversity Trainers in which they were peer educators and changemakers. I was fortunate to know Grayson and request that he share his experience and expertise to educate a hundred members of the Diversity Trainers. By being themselves and being outspoken advocates for acceptance and social justice, all of the student leaders had a positive influence on school culture through peer education, art, theater and new course offerings. Alise, Grayson, Helen and Soul are all socially conscious and taking action to liberate themselves and others to make the world a better place. May their words inspire you to do the same. Enjoy the company of fellow difference-makers as you learn more about yourself, reflect on social systems and craft your social justice project.

Why leadership by young people matters

People of all ages can and do make meaningful contributions. Youth leadership matters because young people can offer different perspectives, dynamic ideas and innovative solutions which challenge assumptions, existing structures and policies to change for the better. As we work towards creating a world that supports all people in achieving their purpose and potential, we must include, center and amplify the voices of young people. How can we collaborate to create sustainable futures? Young people have a vested interest in making necessary changes so we all can live fully.

Young people have made such a difference in my life. I love collaborating with student leaders, seeing them in action and holding space for them to show up in creative and exciting ways. No matter how old you are, you can make a difference!

What is this book about?

Woven throughout the book are stories and perspectives from Alise, Grayson, Helen and Soul related to the big ideas of each chapter. In Chapter 1, we will officially meet the interviewees and consider our own identities, experiences and passions. We'll think about techniques to notice and neutralize shame and stigma because we are all inherently worthy and enough. We'll focus on self-love and encourage affirming self-talk.

In Chapter 2, we'll think about making a difference using language and body-based practices and consider some things to do and avoid for acceptance and social justice.

Chapter 3 focuses on motivation, privilege and acceptance, and includes an activity to counteract stereotypes and assumptions about social groups.

Chapter 4 is a rainbow of goodness! First, we spotlight the Rainbow Dance for LGBTQ+ young people as a featured project, then we reflect on how we transform towards healing and liberation. We get to enjoy a visualization with the colors of the rainbow.

In Chapter 5, we consider building support systems and taking ally action. We practice using gender-neutral pronouns.

Chapter 6 highlights ways we take care of ourselves and acknowledges ways we make a difference.

Chapter 7 expands further on ideas of support and includes holding space for a person who has experienced challenges related to oppression. We will consider actions and statements that are supportive or are less than supportive. We'll role-play conversations with family and friends. We will also think about our role models and the future.

In Chapter 8, we invoke the world of our dreams! We consider areas of concern and improvement, and continue our efforts from Chapter 3 to release negative social messages. We will also think about best practices like consent and transformative justice, decide if a practice is useful for helping or harming and then create a "house of transformation/liberation"!

Chapter 9 includes another featured project which is a youth-led diversity training program. We will focus on actions we can take as we think about dismantling patriarchy, white supremacy and other systems of injustice.

The culminating chapter, Chapter 10, offers an opportunity to bring your social justice action plan into being by identifying your skills, commitments, interests, focus topics, strengths and needed resources as well as encouragement to ensure the accessibility of your project. Stay motivated with a chart to track your progress! Get your love in action to make a difference! Who can be the difference for social justice? You!

A note about terms and concepts

Language changes over time. Usage and understandings evolve, including the ways we name our identities and experiences. In this book, the acronym BIPOC will refer to people in the United States who are Black, Indigenous and people of color. While the term BIPOC seems to indicate a generalized experience, there are significant differences in cultures and in the ways that people are harmed by white supremacy. The term "marginalized" refers to people and groups whose identities and experiences are not centered and who are often excluded by society. People of various sexualities and genders are represented using the term LGBTQ+ (lesbian, gay, bisexual, transgender, queer; the plus includes people who are intersex, asexual, non-binary, gender diverse, Two Spirit, pan/polysexual, and so much more). The singular gender-neutral pronoun "they" is also used throughout the book. This book uses language that is in current use at the time of publication. If the words used seem outdated or do not represent your experience or understandings, just cross them out and write in what is most current or what suits you (well, except for the interviewee's personal identities—please respect those even if there are different identifiers in the future).

Content warnings

As injustice is often correlated with personal and communal suffering, a trauma-sensitive and resilience-oriented care perspective will be woven throughout the book. Looking at oppression can be upsetting and unsettling. Realizing the extent of the harm can feel overwhelming. These are not easy topics. However, it is essential that we develop our consciousness about the many forms of domination (such as racism, sexism, homophobia, transphobia, ableism, saneism and the ways these experiences can overlap) so that we can challenge and change these harmful systems. In consideration for people who have experienced trauma, there will be content warnings in this book just before sections that include common stressors using this format:

R = Racism

S = Sexism

H = Homophobia

T = Transphobia

L = Language that is considered harmful

/ = Warning end

Combinations of those will be noted as well, such as SH for sexism and homophobia. A slash / signals the end of the concerning section. Other content may also be upsetting. If at any time you find that you are having a reaction, please put the book down and take care of yourself.

The interviews were conducted virtually on video chat during the spring of 2020 in the midst of the global pandemic, which has intensified and worsened systemic injustices for marginalized groups in terms of health, housing and economic status. Concerns about the impact of Covid-19 will be mentioned in the interviews.

You rock!

Thank you for bringing your full self to the experience of this book. Whenever possible, please integrate the practices into your everyday life.

May you find joy, learning and liberation in the activities and interviews, and in the process of creating your own social justice project. May you recognize your greatness and your power, and find new and exciting ways to challenge injustice and dismantle oppression with the help of this book. May you experience respite (a much-needed break), sanctuary (a nurturing haven), recognition of your efforts and inspiration in this space. You are welcome here. All aspects of your identity are honored, appreciated and needed here. Your experiences and passions are essential. You are completely accepted for all of who you are.

CHAPTER 1
IDENTITIES AND STIGMA AND SHAME, OH MY!

Are you ready to be introduced to the featured interviewees? I'm so excited for you to meet them! Let's learn a bit about each of the interviewees in their own words and voices. We'll read about their social justice passions a little later in the chapter. You'll also have an opportunity to reflect on your own identities and experiences.

For extended versions of the interviews as well as image descriptions, please visit https://library.jkp.com/redeem using the code TJNMTUC

Alise

I'm Alise Mackey. My pronouns are she, her and hers. I just turned 18. I'm Black. That's a really big part of my identity. Being a part of a Black family has just been my identity since I can remember. And I'm a woman. Those are the two identities that are really close to my heart right now. Those two intersections have been difficult to navigate in a lot of different spaces. I think there are a lot of moments where I have to choose

what's more salient—well, what people see more—and it's been a bit of a frustration for me, especially in activism. People are constantly having to choose: "Am I Black or am I a woman?" Which is not really a choice that should be forced on anyone at all. But it's something that I've had to navigate a little bit and I've been lucky to have space to think about it, people to talk to about it and people who have supported me.

Grayson

My name is Grayson Ray. I am 17, almost 18 years old, I'm a queer trans man, and I use he/him and they/them pronouns. My identity as a trans person is something I do feel is vital to who I am. My growth towards getting involved in activism for my community and, more personally, loving and accepting myself has been one of the hardest but most liberating things I have ever done. The struggles I faced after coming out and how I combatted them are a huge part of my character. Today, I feel proud of who I am.

Helen

My name is Helen Everbach. I use all gender pronouns and don't have a particular preference about pronouns. I am 20 years old. I have a number of identities that are marginalized by society. To begin with, I'm a woman, although that identity is more a political than personal one. I kind of stopped seeing the usefulness of a gender identity for myself once I learned more about gender in an academic setting and realized the whole thing is socially created and defined, but I do find it occasionally politically useful to be able to call myself a woman. I'm white and grew up pretty privileged as upper middle class. I'm queer and femme but I'm still pretty visibly queer and quite open about that identity. I'm also kinky and non-monogamous and I am a practitioner of Unitarian Universalism. I have also struggled with mental health challenges for many years. I am in college. I'm a feminist studies and literature double major. I'm a playwright and that's my main form of art activism. In terms of activism outside the art world, I work with a group that does peer-to-peer sex education on campus. I design workshops and I also work as a research assistant in a lab that studies sexual diversity.

Soul

I am Soul Cooke. My pronouns are fae/faer/fen or they/ their/them and I am 23 years old. I'm non-binary and genderqueer. I also recently came across gender creative and that suits me as well. I came out before they/their/ them was widely accepted and in the dictionary as a singular pronoun. There was, at one point, a really huge pushback against non-binary people using they/their/ them. It doesn't seem that complicated for us to switch  to a society where we use more than three singular pronouns being she/ her, he/him, they/them. How to use the pronouns fae/faer/fen is also important so more people can be comfortable with it and more people I'm close to can use it. I'm queer and asexual and I ran the meet-up for asexuals at a national Trans Wellness Conference one year, opening with the question, "What is this thing called sexual attraction?" We had in-depth conversations led by smaller groups of individuals, which I found really meaningful. I'm actually incredibly proud of the poem I wrote to get into art school, which said "I AM" and then was just a whole list of things that I am: a Unitarian Universalist, a feminist, autistic, genderqueer, not my mother's daughter—'cause I'm not a daughter. It ended with, "And I didn't wear it for you." It is still a beautiful poem that I adore and am so proud of.

Reflection: Big ideas from interviewees

What most intrigues you about what Alise, Grayson, Helen and Soul shared?

....

....

....

Alise talks about the intersections of her identities. Intersectionality is a term that was crafted in 1989 by Civil Rights scholar and law professor Kimberlé Crenshaw to help us understand that when multiple identities are marginalized, the effects of disadvantage or discrimination are compounded. For example, racialized sexism compounds the harms of sexism for Black women which non-Black women are not likely to experience or experience differently. Characterizations of Black women as angry, sassy, strong or sexualized are used to deny pain and mistreatment and contribute to a lack of care and support.[1] This is called misogynoir, a term coined by author Moya Bailey in 2008 to help us recognize and work towards changing the types of racialized sexism Black women face.[2]

Helen describes gender as "socially created and defined." That's a great way to explain the concept of a social construct. In his book *My Grandmother's Hands: Racialized Trauma and the Pathway to Mending our Hearts and Bodies* (2017), author and embodied antiracist culture-builder Resmaa Menakem explains that "race is a myth with teeth and claws."[3] Categories like race and gender have been used to divide people and uphold structures of power and profit. Who benefits from these structures and who is harmed?

. . . .

. . . .

. . . .

Who are you?

Soul describes and shares part of the "I AM" poem which fae wrote for faer college application. An "I AM" poem is such a wonderful way to acknowledge the many aspects of our identities and some of the complexities of our experiences. When we recognize how multi-dimensional we are, it helps us realize that there are many facets to each person. We cannot put people in tidy boxes with a single identity label. As Alise shared, there may be one identity that people see as more prominent but that is not the whole truth and that can feel restricting or limiting. As Black lesbian poet, author and professor Audre Lorde reminds us, "we do not lead single issue lives."[4] Can we recognize the full humanity of people by remembering complexity? To do that, we can start by honoring ourselves in our own beautiful complexities.

For this activity, use the letters of the alphabet to stimulate your thinking about your own identities and experiences. Generate the list by starting in alphabetical order or by randomly writing in your identities/experiences. Have fun with it! Feel free to write more than one word for each letter. You could also write phrases. If you would enjoy creating this list as quickly as possible, give yourself 15 minutes. If you prefer an unlimited amount of time, just let yourself feel into all of your aspects. There is no need to rush. You could keep coming back to this exercise over the next few days or next few years!

Here are a few prompts to get you started. Pick and choose the ones that you feel moved to express. Who are you? Who do you love (including animals)? Where do you live? Who do you live with? How old are you? What do you like to do? Do you have a favorite place in nature? Do you have a favorite color, food, location, book, subject, show, movie, music or pastime/sport? Where are your people from (if known)? What is your culture, race/ethnicity or tribal affiliation (if any)? What language(s) do you speak or sign? Does your family speak or sign other languages? What is your learning style (spatial, bodily kinesthetic, musical, linguistic, logical-mathematical, interpersonal, intrapersonal and/or naturalistic)?[5] What are you passionate about? How do you identify your: gender identity and gender expression; sexual orientation; romantic orientation; religion/spirituality; socio-economic status; family configuration (given or chosen); current status of health, mental/behavioral health, neurodiversity and disability/ability; personality type; relationship preference; and political affiliation?

I AM:

A ....

B ....

C ....

D ....

E ....

F ....

G ....

H ....

I ....

J ....

K ....

L ....

M ....

N ....

O ....

P ....

Q ....

R ....

S ....

T ....

U ....

V ....

W ....

X ....

Y ....

Z ....

Create your I AM expression!

Now that you have this awesome list, what would you like to do with it? Here are some options: draw or paint a picture; write a story, song, rap or poem; create a collage; dance it; or use a combination of methods. For example, you could create a performance art piece with spoken word and movement and record your performance on video! You could embellish the poem with drawings around the edges or through and around the words. You could take photos of people, places and things that inspire you or remind you of the words/identities/experiences and create a visual presentation to share with friends and family. However you would like to express yourself, have fun with the creation process! You may use this space, your journal, a canvas or another medium of your choice.

I AM:

Let's hear from Alise, Grayson, Helen and Soul now as they each address the question "What are you **passionate** about?"

Alise

I'm passionate about criminal justice injustices and families and trauma. I think that it's always been present in my family and in my mind that I need to act a certain way when I'm in a certain place. My mother always told me to be twice as good, especially going to school, to be on my best behavior, to try to be as good as I can— just the whole respectability politics type of stuff that young kids are taught all the time. It was the same with my brother, too, talking about dealing with police, dealing with things that kids shouldn't really have to deal with. I remember my brother and my dad joking about driving while Black and being pulled over, and they would joke about it because that's how we deal with things, with a lot of humor. Seeing all this criminal justice injustice on social media has been super hard-hitting in a really big place of passion for me because I see my brothers and sisters in these victims all the time. That could have been my sister. That could have been my dad. And so, I think a lot of these issues for me cause a lot of anxiety. I conducted my year-long Advanced Placement research project on how police brutality is portrayed in the media and how victim-blaming rhetoric affects viewers' interpretations of crimes that are committed. I got to see some things come to life in the data that even my teacher didn't really believe. So it was, I guess, gratifying, but also not gratifying to see a really sad hypothesis become true. These passions are really draining sometimes.

Grayson

I'm very passionate about equality and social justice for every oppressed group. My main passion is creating social change for the transgender community in particular. My passions mostly lie in spreading education about my community, my identity, my experiences and other people's stories in my community, to people who are not inside the community, because the transgender community is often overlooked, even in many "activist" spaces. A lot of people don't even know that trans people exist. There is a lot more to be done in the realm of education. So that's my goal, my passion, what I'm working towards.

Helen

Sexuality in general is my main leading passion in life. I feel so lucky that I was raised a Unitarian Universalist because I grew up in a religious community that thinks about sexuality in a way that most communities don't. I was never taught to think about my body or my sexuality with shame. And I understand that that's a privilege that most people in the United States don't have. So I really want to get through to people that no matter what the experiences that you might have had with sexuality and whatever your desires are, they're okay. If you can safely enact them with a consenting, sober partner, do that. I'm also passionate about a play I've recently written that some friends and I are trying to produce as a web series since we can't produce it as a play in person because of the Covid-19 outbreak. I'm quite excited about adapting this lesbian erotica-like gay sex comedy into a web series format. I focus on looking at the particular issues, concerns and challenges of dealing with mental health, gender, sexuality, but also patriarchy and what it means to be intimate with others as a queer woman.

Soul

I have always been passionate about sharing myself. I am passionate about my Bachelor of Fine Arts (BFA) show "Entire Unto Myself" [December 2019]. It really was such a magical day.

One piece is of a hundred cast-glass flower bouquets. They're very intricately colored in yellows and pinks and very layered. What makes this a very special piece is it's arranged in the shape of my scars as if I'm standing in the center of the room. I've done some other kinds of disability-related work and some of it involves my head, my face, casting it in glass. I also have a piece that I displayed at the Glass Art Society student exhibition called "In Honor of the Favorite Dog Toy," which was when I was training a service dog. My work at the time really revolved around respecting dogs, training and helping dogs and sharing information about how to succeed, advocacy and thoughts around expanding the programs which provide service dogs, and educating about the laws protecting the service dog team. I would not have been on a waiting list for a service dog if I hadn't developed a heart condition. And if it wasn't for that, I could not have gotten the service dog I needed.

I'm passionate about quite a few things. One is really related to this experience we're all having with Covid-19. I had a surprisingly hard time with it in the beginning, considering that my daily life wasn't disrupted. I'm a homebody. I don't have a service dog right now. So, I can't leave the house and really do things by myself so much. I came to a good conclusion about it with my therapist, which was very reassuring because part of self-care is accepting your emotions and turning to them and saying, "Yes, this, this, too." And I could accept and forgive myself for feeling this way. So, I've been editing a couple of different videos right now, which include me talking about the hurdles that I ran into in the work that I did for my BFA show: here's what I'm overcoming; how did I make this beautiful thing that I love, that I adore; how did I make it happen? I hope that I'm capturing the same sort of calmness, the same sort of uplifting feelings that creators in the historical costuming world who really helped me out of my rut shared through their videos. But even if it's just soothing and just helping someone day-to-day who can't find that creative energy but at least isn't alone, that's really important to me.

Reflection: What are you passionate about?

What most resonates with you about what Alise, Grayson, Helen and Soul shared about their passions? What are you passionate about?

. . . .

. . . .

. . . .

Internalized oppression

Helen shares, "I never was taught to think about my body or my sexuality with shame." That's awesome! Many of us do hold shame (and that's nothing to be ashamed about!). Let's consider how social forces operate on us personally and how we can challenge default thinking.

We often experience social pressures to appear a certain way or act a certain way. Alise shares her experience with "respectability politics," which is an expression attributed to African American history and religion professor Evelyn Brooks Higginbotham, Ph.D., to indicate the pressure to conform to the dominant culture's expectations of "good" behavior, language and dress/appearance with the hope of acceptance and protection from discrimination.

Have you ever felt you had to change yourself to "fit in"?

❏   Yes

❏   No

❏   I'm not sure

If you answered yes, what was the reason? Terms naming that oppression are listed in brackets. (Check all that apply ✓.)

❏   My age [ageism]

❏   My culture or immigration status [xenophobia]

❏   My skin color or physical features [racism/racialization, white supremacy, colorism]

❏   My/family's income, housing, education level [classism]

❏   My religion [religious bias]

❏   My ability/disability [ableism]

❏   My body size [sizeism])

❏   My health status [health bias]

- ❏ My mental health status [saneism]

- ❏ The way my mind works [neurodiversity bias]

- ❏ My sexual orientation [homophobia, biphobia, queerphobia]

- ❏ My gender identity and/or gender expression (my style of clothes/hair/voice/mannerisms) [sexism, transphobia, gender binary bias]

- ❏ My family situation

- ❏ Another reason (specify): ....

Why do/did you feel you needed to change? (Check as many as apply ✓.)

- ❏ I want(ed) to be liked

- ❏ I do/did not feel safe being fully myself

- ❏ I am/was embarrassed about the way(s) I am different from others/the dominant culture

- ❏ Bullying

- ❏ I want(ed) to look like images in the media

- ❏ Peer pressure

- ❏ I want(ed) to be like "everyone else"

- ❏ I do/did not want to be judged

- ❏ I have/had a hard time accepting/liking/loving myself

- ❏ Another reason (specify): ....

Hazardous social programming

This activity is intended as a tool. If you or someone you care about needs help, please seek and connect with (professional) support.

How are shame and stigma related to oppression? There are a variety of reasons why people might have negative messages playing in their minds, including social programming. Author and professor Ibram X. Kendi, Ph.D., helps us recognize "the consistent function of racist ideas—and of any kind of bigotry more broadly: to manipulate us into seeing people as the problem, instead of the policies that ensnare them."[6] When we see ourselves and other people as "the problem," we are subject to further manipulation by those who seek to exploit our vulnerabilities for profit or power.

Consider how we are constantly bombarded with advertising that we are not good enough, not a certain "ideal" body size, in need of products, services or surgeries to achieve a certain look or appeal to potential mates. Why are we not enough just as we are? In her book *The Body is Not an Apology: The Power of Radical Self-Love*, Sonya Renee Taylor calls this harmful system the "Body-Shame Profit Complex"[7] and reminds us to question and challenge thinking, messages, images, policies and institutions that uphold some bodies as supreme and others as unworthy.

Disability justice writer and educator Mia Mingus offers an in-depth explanation of the ills of the Medical Industrial Complex. She writes,

> It is a system about profit, first and foremost, rather than 'health,' well being and care. Its roots run deep and its history and present are connected to everything including eugenics, capitalism, colonization, slavery, immigration, war, prisons, and reproductive oppression.[8]

Who might profit financially from our self-defeating thoughts ("I'm not...enough")?

a. The diet industry

b. The beauty industry

c. The Medical Industrial Complex

d. All of the above

[Answer: d]

Who benefits from our healing, empowerment and our acceptance of ourselves? We do.

How can we be fully ourselves, fully accepting of ourselves, compassionate and loving towards ourselves and others? What needs to happen to create that space in our bodies and in society?

We have been constantly exposed to social systems that are based on centering and upholding certain people as more intelligent, more beautiful, more powerful, more deserving and somehow better or even more human when compared to other people who are somehow less than or deserving of less. Those ideas are not true. Who profits/benefits from white supremacy? Whose continued positions of power are maintained and at whose expense? Ask these questions of all social systems and institutions. Sonya Renee Taylor reminds us that:

> Racism, sexism, ableism, homo- and transphobia, ageism, fatphobia are algorithms created by humans' struggle to make peace with the body. A radical self-love world is a world free from the systems of oppression that make it difficult and sometimes deadly to live in our bodies.[9]

How have our cultures, minds and bodies been shaped and informed by the dominant culture? Let's think about how negative programming sounds in ourselves and then we'll consider how we might respond when we hear or see our friends, family or community members engaging with this programming.

What messages have we received that tell us we are "too much" or "not good enough"?

Negative self-talk

Words and statements with negative associations will be considered in the next text box so they can be identified and released. Please work with a professional or other trusted source as needed.

Judging or criticizing yourself might sound like:

I'm too .... (negative idea)

I'm not .... enough

Who I am is not okay

I can't ....

I hate .... (aspect of self)

I wish I wasn't ....

I'm a bad ....

Other negative self-talk might involve comparing yourself to others, thinking it is all your fault (blaming yourself) or expecting the worst to happen.

Write any other negative self-talk which you are aware you say/think:

....

....

/ ....

Where did those ideas come from? (Check as many as apply ✓.)

❏ My parent(s)/guardian(s)

❏ My relative(s)

❏ My friend(s)

❏ Someone I am/was dating

❏ My school

- ❏ My religion/culture

- ❏ My community

- ❏ Medical professional(s)

- ❏ Law enforcement

- ❏ Historical events

- ❏ Social media

- ❏ Advertising, TV, movies, radio, books

- ❏ A lack of (positive) representation in media and leadership

- ❏ I'm not sure (I'll think on it)

- ❏ A different source (specify): ....

The point of identifying the source is not to assign blame but rather to question whether it was your own original thought and if you can let it go.

Please do not be upset with yourself for having negative self-talk. Please do not blame yourself as that can create another layer of shame. It's not your fault! You are not alone. Lots of people have these thoughts. Most of us have received messages that we are "not okay/enough" so that we will be distracted from addressing human rights injustices and environmental issues. Remember that it takes time and consistent practice to liberate ourselves from a lifetime of social programming. Be patient with yourself.

Just observe the words/thoughts you say to yourself. Recording your observation is a powerful way to begin to unpack the thought/statement. In a loving, non-judgmental way, ask yourself:

- What's going on with me?
- Where did these thoughts come from?
- Are they serving me?

Mindfully witness yourself. You may not be conscious of these thoughts or they may be a habit. Bring your awareness to the thoughts. These thoughts may arise or be activated by circumstances. Have compassion for yourself. We will flag them, neutralize or divert them, repair and replace them.

The shame and stigma shut down

Let's create a container for self-awareness and transformation. Look at the negative self-talk or self-defeating thought. Notice its color, texture, volume, energy. See it for all it is. Feel it in your body. Notice its effect. Don't get stuck there! Now let's imagine a door or a window opening through which to let in a fresh gentle breeze and release the negative self-talk/thought. We witness and bring love to ourselves.

Let's create new pathways and offer ourselves healing in places where negative social programming has become automatic. Redirect yourself gently as a kind caregiver would for a child or a sweet puppy.

Which of the following images or tools resonate with you for flagging negative self-talk? Put a plus sign (+) next to any item you would like to try. Put a star/asterisk (*) next to the one you would like to work with immediately.

- ❏ Catcher's mitt
- ❏ Color flag or sticker
- ❏ Divert the delivery notice
- ❏ Do not cross tape
- ❏ Do not enter sign
- ❏ Flashing lights
- ❏ Hazardous/toxic materials sign
- ❏ Hear the Supremes' song "Stop! In the Name of Love"
- ❏ Highlight or glow-light
- ❏ Junk mail folder
- ❏ "No, thanks"

- ❏ "Not mine"

- ❏ Push the pause button

- ❏ Put the brakes on

- ❏ Railroad track switch

- ❏ Refused

- ❏ Return to sender

- ❏ Road block

- ❏ Shut it down! (Push the button or pull the lever)

- ❏ Spam filter

- ❏ Stop sign

- ❏ Undeliverable

- ❏ Unwanted message notice

- ❏ Use a butterfly net (for fleeting thoughts/ideas)

- ❏ Warning!

- ❏ Wash it away

- ❏ "Welcome. Goodbye."

- ❏ Another option: . . . .

Fill in the blank with the description of the item you prioritized above with a star/asterisk (*):

When I notice myself having thoughts, behavior and/or using language or images that are less than respectful of myself or people with whom I have a common identity, I will:

. . . .

. . . .

. . . .

You could also say to yourself:

- "Oh, interesting. I just had a negative self-talk moment."
- "Look at that thought."
- "I heard that."
- "I'm noticing a reaction."

And then record the statement or just bring your awareness to an option for a remedy. The book *My Anxiety Handbook: Getting Back on Track* includes a process for "catching" and "challenging" our thoughts and features a helpful chart to record and explore the thinking, including creating "a more accurate or helpful thought."[10] Let's explore the idea of more helpful thoughts now.

Positive self-talk

How often do we have negative thoughts about ourselves? Let's ensure that we consciously offer ourselves at least that many affirming statements. Go for twice as many affirming statements! Sometimes it's hard for people to say these statements or believe these statements. Start small. Go slowly. Build up your stamina. If you would like to imagine a kind and caring person is saying these things to you, adapt the statement (for example: "I like you. You are powerful."). While you are saying the words, offer yourself a gesture of physical support such as a hand on the heart or belly or back (or whatever is physically available to you). Remember, you are inherently worthy of love, care and support.

- I like myself
- I love myself
- I love myself just as I am
- I am enough
- I am worthy
- I am strong
- I am powerful
- I am . . . . (affirming word) enough

- I can .... (action word)
- I am safe
- I am abundant
- I have resources
- I am perfectly imperfect
- I love my body
- I take care of myself
- I cherish my heart
- I cherish my ....
  (name an attribute like creativity or body part like hands)
- I am grateful for ....
  (my attribute, my body, people in my life, animals, nature, food,
  shelter, water, the planet, etc.)

The love bathing technique

Awakened/Spiritual intuitive guide, coach and energy healer Shea
Maultsby shares that self-love is a powerful technology. She encourages
us to practice "love bathing" by saying aloud the statement: "I love you
.... (my name), ... (my name),
I love you."[11] Repeat it three times in a row or three times over the course
of the day. Practice it daily if possible. Look in the mirror and into your own
eyes while saying it for a gentle flow of self-love.

Here are some other great strategies to practice to lean into self-love.
Put a plus sign (+) next to any item you would like to try. Put a star/asterisk
(*) next to the one you would like to work with immediately. Put a check
mark (✓) next to any practices you already use.

- ❏ Breathe mindfully

- ❏ Connect with an animal/pet

- ❏ Connect with a person or people who remind you of your greatness

- ❏ Express your gratitude

- ❏ Hold a crystal

❏ Feel the energy in your feet and hands

❏ Get into nature or visualize yourself in a natural setting

❏ Give yourself an affirmation

❏ Hum

❏ Look at your hands

❏ Love yourself even more

❏ Notice the space you are in and focus on something you love

❏ Praise yourself: "Good work!" "Great job!" "You are really doing great!" "Congratulations!"

❏ Say words out loud like "love", "peace" or "harmony"

❏ Sing a lullaby or calming song to yourself

❏ Soothe with water (drink it, bathe in it, be near or visualize a waterfall, the ocean or other body of water)

❏ Tell yourself a new story

❏ Think the best of yourself

❏ Touch the earth or ground

❏ Visualize receiving (giving yourself) a bouquet of flowers

❏ Write in: ....

Put it all together!

When I realize/become aware that my thoughts are disrespectful towards myself or going down a worrying path, I interrupt using (choice from "The shame and stigma shut down" activity):

....

Then I give myself an affirmation or use a self-love strategy (write it here):

....

And offer myself a gesture of physical support (describe it here):

. . . .

Please come back to this practice throughout this book and in your everyday life.

Free(ing) dance!

Let's move our bodies to affirm all the amazing things about ourselves. We are truly incredible beings! Every body is a good body! Watch Mona Haydar's music video "Good Body."[12] Every breath is a good breath. Be creative in your movement. Every movement is beautiful. Release judgment and shame about movement. There are no "bad" or "wrong" moves. If you have been shamed for your body or your movement, shake that off and sweep/whisk it away from you. It's not the truth. It's not yours. This is a dance for liberation! Feel truly free to express yourself through movement. If you can move in new ways, you may learn something or feel a bit different. If you feel self-conscious in a way that makes you uncomfortable, just notice that. It's okay to stop and it's okay to go on if you feel you want to keep trying. Give yourself an affirmation. Put on music and sing out loud if you are so moved. Say your affirmation silently or out loud. Your movement could be slow and meditative like swaying from side to side or rotating. It could be big, bold and exuberant like skipping or jumping. It could be movement in just one body part such as a finger or hand or foot or neck. Your movement could be lying on the floor or ground. It could be standing still and feeling the movement of your lungs rising and falling. There are no rules except to listen to your body and be safe.

Take as much or as little time as you want with this movement experiment. It could be one minute or one hour. Bliss out! Enjoy your body and movement. How does it feel in your body?

Free(ing) dance experience journal

How did that movement experiment go for you? Was it freeing? Did you feel super self-conscious? How did your body feel before and after the movement? Were you able to release any tension? Were there any places in your body that needed attention? What was your affirmation?

Write about any of these ideas or anything else you want to note about your experience:

. . . .

. . . .

. . . .

Consider expanding what you watch and read so that you get a sense of the beauty of all bodies and identities beyond the dominant culture's norms and expectations. Helen shares:

> Diversify your media consumption so that the people you're seeing in the media you're consuming aren't all the same body type, race, binary gender, ability, and so on. Seeing happy, sexy, empowered people with bodies and identities outside the scope of Hollywood-approved beauty standards can really help to feel less like an outsider.

I hear you!

When you hear a friend, family member, loved one (or perhaps a classmate, co-worker, acquaintance or even a stranger) make a statement about themselves that represents negative self-talk, consider gently asking them one of these questions:

- Why do you say that?
- Is that what you believe about yourself?
- What's going on with you?

- Where did that statement come from?
- Is that thought serving your empowerment and/or healing?

Encourage them to make a positive statement to themselves or to say an affirmation. Ask them if they would like to receive an encouraging word from you in addition to their own gentle words. Keep in mind, it is possible that the person may not appreciate you bringing awareness to their negative self-talk and it may be awkward or uncomfortable. It is always your choice to notice and walk away. It might help to preface the question by letting the person know that you are creating healthier self-talk for yourself. "I'm working on noticing the ways I think about myself. Would you mind if I asked you a question about what you just said?" Be open to the possibility that the answer is "no" or "not right now." Breathe into acceptance and allowing.

If someone in your life is consistently putting you or themselves down, it may be necessary to set boundaries with the person. It's okay to ask them to be mindful of their impact or take some space for yourself. Please reach out for support as needed. You deserve care and love.

CHAPTER 2
MAKING A
DIFFERENCE

Let's learn how Alise, Grayson, Helen and Soul **make a difference** and if they have experienced roadblocks or setbacks. Then we'll explore a few activities about actions, assumptions and language.

Alise

I make a difference by connecting with friends who have more diverse backgrounds and are dealing with institutional issues, through my political activism as the press director of the High School Democrats, and through playwriting. Right now, I'm working on a play about what allyship looks like, what unjust systems look like, and how families are really devastated by unjust systems. I interned for a political candidate in  my sophomore year of high school. The issues that mattered most to me were civil rights, reproductive rights, economic inequality, racial inequality, environmental racism and the Green New Deal. The internship was really gratifying because I did believe in a lot of the things that the candidate campaigned about and I just felt super empowered with voter outreach and data entry. I think sometimes it's really hard as young people to feel we're making a difference. At least it is for me. I just feel, "Is what I'm doing actually sustainable? Am I actually doing anything?" I feel my actions have been trial and error, just trying to do what I can and doing things that motivate me and excite me and make me feel as if I'm doing change.

Grayson

I live by the use of education as a tool for creating change and building empathy. You get people to listen and you have the world in your hands, really. You find your platform, you share your voice, you get a community behind you and you change the world. I began by spreading education through presentations in my high school classes, then to larger groups of students such as clubs, and eventually expanded into speaking to hospitals and conferences. I made a presentation to at least a hundred teachers, faculty, administrators and guidance counselors in my junior year about my experiences as a trans student. In classes that I took following my presentation, the teachers started asking for pronouns and using more inclusive language. When I helped with the freshman orientation in my senior year, our principal introduced himself with pronouns and that's one of the big things that I touched on in my presentation. It was a moment for me when I just kind of realized, "Wow! I created difference." Finding my voice, and having my voice fostered by others, has been one of the most empowering experiences of my life. All LGBTQ+ people deserve to feel empowered and powerful.

At the beginning of my coming-out journey there were a lot of setbacks. And every time that something in politics happens that negatively affects my community or other marginalized communities, those are setbacks. But there are always ways to fight against that. And that starts with education and organizing.

Helen

I think my identities pushed me to make a difference, as a gay Unitarian Universalist. From the Unitarian Universalist sex education program, I learned that bodies are different, and that's okay. And you can have a loving family that looks a lot of different ways, and that's okay, too. I found that that was a good background to have as a young queer person. At school, I shared the things I'd learned at church and answered questions, and so I began my journey making a difference as a sex educator. That's when I really got into activism, started learning about different sexual orientations, getting involved in gender politics, and definitely just becoming more political. All through middle school and high school, I was very involved in telling people off for using language that was harmful. I remember a moment when I must have been in seventh grade where a classmate in science class said a film was gay. He said, "That's so gay." And then I said, "How is a film gay? That's a slur." And I continued to educate people about sex, which was always an interest of mine. In high school, I even formed a club and basically wrote my own sex education curriculum. In college, I've continued running workshops and doing peer-to-peer sex education. It's irritating because there's a lot of pushback against doing work in education for sexuality. Yet there's so much evidence that it's necessary. There's an epidemic of sexual violence on college campuses, but a lot of people don't want to think about it. They think it's personal and private and shouldn't be something that we talk about openly. I get so frustrated, because I think it's so useful to learn about these things, for risk prevention and even just to encourage people to have better sex and explore their bodies and have a better relationship with sex. A lot of people don't feel particularly good about their sex lives and their bodies. There's a lot of shame and stigma that people have internalized. I would love for people to have good sex. That's a great goal.

Soul

One thing I'm pretty proud of and I've been focusing on more recently is the comic that I started called *Just Make It (Through)*—meaning just make art, but also, just get through this. I enjoy showing that this is what life is like as a disabled person, as someone with a service dog, as someone who doesn't look disabled. I took a class on disability and did an ADA (Americans with Disabilities Act) survey of my university campus as a project. I felt

that I was doing my part as someone who literally took a class and someone who is a part-time wheelchair user, part-time cane user. I would get so mad at people locking their bikes to the accessibility rail when I started using a wheelchair and needed to be wheeled to student health to recover from my seizures. The bikes were just in the way. We couldn't get past them.

I'm sure there have been some challenges and setbacks, but I don't really focus on them. One thing that I have an incredibly hard time shaking off is when people say mean things to me online. That consistently hurts me and is difficult to deal with. Everything else is a mental challenge that I can get through and I have the tools to get through and I'm excited to get through. I don't think about things as setbacks, but my response is to find it kind of intellectually stimulating, and as problem solving, and I embrace that.

Reflection: Making a difference

What stands out to you most as you reflect on what Alise, Grayson, Helen and Soul shared about some of the ways they make a difference? What are some of the ways you make a difference?

. . . .

. . . .

. . . .

Dance it out!

Grayson says, "You find your platform, you share your voice, you get a community behind you and you change the world." If you are able and willing, let's do a little dance inspired by Grayson's words and his coronation as Homecoming King (discussed more in Chapter 4)! Use these ideas or create your own images and expressions.

1. Channel regal energy: hands above your head as if you are placing a crown.
2. Find your platform/stage: take a few powerful steps (enter the stage, walk the runway!).
3. Share your voice: hands cupped as megaphone or hand(s) on microphone.
4. Change the world: hands circling as spheres.

Now put on your favorite music and have fun! Play with joining the four movements together and try them in sequence in four directions. Add in any additional moves that are meaningful to you. Imagine your audience (if that's fun for you). What is your message?

. . . .

. . . .

. . . .

Can we recognize actions and attitudes that are things to do and things to avoid? Helen describes how she would tell people that the language they were using is harmful. Let's think about assumptions, actions and language in the next few activities.

Do or don't?

How should we respond when connecting with friends, family members, in school, at work or in the community? Decide whether the following items are generally things to do or things not to do. Circle your choice for each item. There may be exceptions or variations for some items depending on the context. Please write a note in the margin or your journal when you think of exceptions. These topics are just a few of many big issues that are often not discussed or officially taught.

No.	Choice	Topic
1.	DO / DON'T	Assume intelligence based on skin color, accent, dialect or English proficiency
2.	DO / DON'T	Ask before touching someone or their belongings
3.	DO / DON'T	Challenge anti-Black racism and all racialization in policy, practice and in your own mind and body
4.	DO / DON'T	Assume a person of marginalized identities wants to answer questions about their body, mind, identity or experience
5.	DO / DON'T	Consider all bodies as good
6.	DO / DON'T	Have visual displays of support (button, bracelet, sign/poster, clothing) such as "queer, trans and non-binary Black Lives Matter" and feature people of all visible differences (skin colors, ages, sizes, abilities, etc.)
7.	DO / DON'T	Consider there are both visible and non-visible disabilities
8.	DO / DON'T	Dismiss concerns by saying, "I didn't mean it," "I was just joking," "We were just playing around," "Get over it," "It's not a big deal" or "Stop being so sensitive"
9.	DO / DON'T	Use representations of Indigenous people as mascots
10.	DO / DON'T	Ask before offering assistance to someone with a visible disability
11.	DO / DON'T	Assume someone is too old or too young to know something or do something
12.	DO / DON'T	Consider that professions/jobs, clothing, hair and toys have no inherent gender association
13.	DO / DON'T	Assume that everyone is straight and/or cisgender until "proven" otherwise. Assume gender and sexual orientation are related
14.	DO / DON'T	Recognize that multiple marginalized identities create layers of risk and stress
15.	DO / DON'T	Use language inclusive of people of all genders (people, folks, friends, students, clients, everyone of all genders, chairperson, they; **instead of** sir/ma'am, boys and girls, ladies and gentlemen, "both genders," chairman, he/she)

cont.

No.	Choice	Topic
16.	DO / DON'T	Use language that does not presume sexual orientation or monogamy such as partner(s), love interest(s), lover(s), relationship(s)
17.	DO / DON'T	Assume health status based on body size
18.	DO / DON'T	Share the name a person was assigned at birth which they no longer use
19.	DO / DON'T	Have limiting expectations about people based on identity or disability
20.	DO / DON'T	Learn more when you are not sure about a cultural norm or social issue
21.	DO / DON'T	Notice patterns of disadvantage and exclusion based on intersecting identities (racialization, gender, socio-economic status, ethnicity, culture, religion, age, sexual orientation, ability, mental/behavioral health, language, etc.) and take action to end or disrupt those patterns
22.	DO / DON'T	Assume that your experience is other people's experience

Are there items or practices on the list which you would like to do more often? Is there something that you want to stop doing now?

. . . .

. . . .

. . . .

Answer key for "Do or don't?"

If you have different answers from what appears in this key, it could be based on interpretation or consideration of context/circumstance.

DO: #2, 3, 5, 6, 7, 10, 12, 14, 15, 16, 20, 21

DON'T: #1, 4, 8, 9, 11, 13, 17, 18, 19, 22

Pronouns

Subject	Object	Possessive
She	Her	Hers
He	Him	His
They	Them	Theirs
Fae	Fen	Faers
Ze	Hir	Hirs

...and more!

Or no pronouns

Helen teaching

One thing most of us need to be mindful of is our language. Let's consider that now.

"That's so..." BLANK

This activity was inspired by Helen and Soul's 2014 training packet for the Diversity Trainers "Recognizing Language that Dehumanizes People."[1]

Language matters. Words are powerful. Many words have current and/or historical connections to oppression. Let's decide if the way these common expressions are used would be classified as neutral, funny, or harmful. Please fill in the blank with the letter **N** for Neutral, **F** for Funny, or **H** for Harmful.

1. . . . . "That's so gay."
2. . . . . "That's so crazy."
3. . . . . "That's so ghetto."
4. . . . . "She's an illegal immigrant."
5. . . . . "You idiot!"
6. . . . . "Did she have a sex-change operation?"
7. . . . . "Don't be such a sissy."
8. . . . . "I'm colorblind to skin color."
9. . . . . "My mom was spazzing out."
10. . . . . "They are terrorists."
11. . . . . "She's wheelchair-bound."
12. . . . . "She's so OCD [obsessive compulsive disorder]."
        "He's so ADHD [attention deficit hyperactivity disorder]."
13. . . . . "Why do those people want special rights?"

Alternative language

Instead of using the above expressions to indicate disapproval or upset at the expense of other people, let's consider some alternatives. Here are some options. Please add your own! Be creative! Help others recognize why you are using an alternative and encourage them to experiment with new options, too. "That's so..."

Bananas	Boring	Intense
Bizarre	Funny	Messed up

Outrageous	Unacceptable	Unfunny
Out there	Unbelievable	Unusual
Perplexing	Uncool	Upsetting
Profound	Unexpected	Zany
Strange	Unfair	

Write in your ideas: . . . .

"'That's so…' BLANK" answer key and discussion

Every one of the 13 common expressions is harmful; none are funny or neutral. Surprised? Some people might say that it depends on the context and the relationship between the people in the conversation. Maybe. Too often, though, people don't realize the way that casual banter perpetuates everyday disrespect, stereotypes and (sometimes subtle) hostility. If a student constantly hears "that's so gay" used as an insult by peers and it is uncorrected by teachers, that creates a culture in which homophobia is accepted, perpetuating stigma and shame.[2] Conversely, accepting teachers, families, social support and safe spaces help promote resiliency for LGBTQ+ teens.[3]

Language that dehumanizes people is so prevalent and so often unexamined! Please do not use slurs or other disrespectful terms regarding culture, race, gender, sexual orientation, cognitive ability, physical ability, mental/behavioral health or any other attribute or identity. Helen describes her efforts to bring awareness to harmful language. Please let others know when their language is hurtful. Keep working to normalize difference in every context.

Let's consider why each common expression is harmful.

1. "That's so gay." It's not okay to use sexual orientation as an insult. Please do not use slurs for LGBTQ+ people. Another common homophobic expression is "no homo" which is a way of distancing oneself from the possibility of being perceived or interpreted

as queer. Would there be a need to say that if queerness was considered an asset?

2. "That's so crazy." How often do you casually hear people say "crazy" or "insane"? All the time, right? This promotes mental/behavioral health stigma. Other examples include: "We had an insane amount of homework" and "He's psycho/schizo/deranged."

3. "That's so ghetto." This is an insult about social class and people who live in areas that are underinvested.

4. "She's an illegal immigrant." No human is illegal. Please use the word undocumented.

5. "You idiot!" Insulting someone's intelligence is not cool and creates a culture of shame and pity towards people with cognitive and/or intellectual disabilities. "That's so r-." The r-slur is also used to insult intelligence.

6. "Did she have a sex-change operation?" Why would someone ask this? Bodies and procedures are really no one's business! If it happens to be necessary information, language that is in current use is gender "affirming/affirmation" or "alignment" or "confirmation" which was previously called "gender transition" (and may still be called that by trans and non-binary people). Please also avoid transphobic language such as: he-she, she-he, it, tranny, trap, and using the past tense "transgendered."

7. "Don't be such a sissy." This demeans traits traditionally associated with femininity and is used to enforce rigid gender norms for men/boys and masculine-identified people. It is an example of femme-phobia.

8. "I'm colorblind to skin color." This is a refusal to acknowledge the harms of racialization by thinking, "I'm not racist. I'm a good person." Most people do perceive differences in skin color and culture. Racial slurs are not acceptable, nor is denial of systemic abuses under white supremacy. It is also considered ableist to use disability references for non-disability issues (color blindness is a way people perceive or do not perceive color).

9. "My mom was spazzing out." This demeans people with certain movement disabilities.

10. "They are terrorists." Targeting someone who is or is thought to be Muslim, Arab or South West Asian/North African is hurtful and perpetuates Islamaphobia.

11. "She's wheelchair-bound." Mobility devices are essential and not to be pitied or stigmatized. Would we say "glasses-bound"? No, we just say, "She wears glasses." It would be better to say, "She uses a wheelchair" or, "She's a wheelchair user." Another common expression to avoid is "that's lame" as it causes stigma towards people with physical/mobility issues. Remember, all bodies are good.

12. "She's so OCD." "He's so ADHD." Embrace neurodiversity. It is not a source of ridicule or shame. Neurodiversity includes autism, ADHD, OCD, dyslexia (letters, symbols, reading) and dyscalculia (number-based calculations).

13. "Why do those people want special rights?" This can be heard in reference to LGBTQ+, BIPOC, and people with disabilities, who refuse to accept disrespectful treatment and discriminatory laws and policies. There are no "special" rights, only human rights. Check out the United Nations *Universal Declaration of Human Rights*.[4]

As Helen and Soul say, "This is not an exhaustive list—there are many, many insulting words/phrases (unfortunately)."[5]

What are some other common expressions or words that dehumanize which you have encountered?

. . . .

. . . .

. . . .

Have you or a person you care about felt upset by common expressions or casual conversations where someone did not realize how hurtful their language was? What was the issue? How did you address it (if at all)?

Did you think it was just your personal issue or did you realize the expression was connected to a larger issue of systemic oppression?

. . . .

. . . .

. . . .

What are some ways to express your concern for hurtful language?

. . . .

. . . .

. . . .

Sometimes it may feel scary to point out language that dehumanizes people. What if the person who is saying something hurtful is your teacher, family member, friend or someone who is perceived as an authority figure? Sometimes we may be stunned into silence. That's why it's good to practice in advance.

When I hear hurtful language, I will say...

Check your favorite response (✓):

- ❏ "That's a stereotype"
- ❏ "That language is hurtful"
- ❏ "That language is hurtful to . . . . people"
- ❏ "Did you know that word/expression is hurtful?"
- ❏ "That word/expression promotes shame"

- ❏ "Is that supposed to be funny?"

- ❏ "What did you say?"

- ❏ "I'm not okay with that word/expression"

- ❏ "That language is not cool"

- ❏ "What do you mean when you say that?"

- ❏ "Did you intend to promote hate?"

- ❏ "That's an insult"

- ❏ "That's insulting"

- ❏ "That causes stigma"

- ❏ "That's a slur"*

- ❏ Write in: ....

Now, say the response you checked five times out loud. Say it quietly. Say it loudly. Say it with conviction. Feel courage and power in your body as you say it. We'll continue practicing in Chapter 7 with role plays about speaking up.

If it doesn't feel right or safe to respond/interrupt/interject/speak up in the moment, you can certainly circle back with the person or people another time. You may need time to pause, breathe and feel before responding. If you have an ally who is willing to step in, this may be a great time to enlist their support.

*As a follow-up to Helen's story about saying, "That's a slur," Helen shares this:

> I do think this tactic works in a blunt sort of way, but I wouldn't recommend it for situations with people you have ongoing relationships with, since it'll likely escalate the situation. This was my go-to tactic in high school and now I tend to pull people aside and start with questions rather than just saying, "That's racist" or whatnot.

Now, let's think about how we can play with words to give them an empowering twist!

Reframe it!

Language is powerful. Naming things gives us new understandings about them. When a word is in use, there is a collective accumulation of experience with that word. Over time, the meanings of words may evolve. Some words have power because of the ways they have been wielded as weapons to keep people down.

Words are tools. Think of a tool like a hammer. It can be used to build a house. It can also be used to tear down or harm. Have you ever accidentally hit your thumb or finger when you were trying to hammer in a nail? That hurts! Was the tool designed with that outcome in mind? Probably not. Let's use our creativity to reframe words to be tools of empowerment.

An acrostic is a way to play with words to create poems or new insights. Take each letter of the word and write it down in a column on the left side of the page. Writer, educator and artist Vanessa Rochelle Lewis uses an acrostic to reframe the word UGLY as:

Uplift

Glorify and

Love

Yourself[6]

She has created a social movement for "a more inclusive, compassionate world where all human bodies and lives are recognized as inherently valuable and worthy of existence, welcome, love, rest, pleasure and protection."[7] Yes, please!

Let's think about a word that is currently used to insult, shame and control, often directed at women. The word is slut. Can we make the letters of that word into an acrostic to reclaim the power that is intended to be seized when the word slut is hurled as an insult?

Let's brainstorm words that have positive connotations starting with the letters s, l, u, t and play around with them in combination.[8]

S: safe, self-assertive, self-confident, sexy, sincere(ly), smart, smiling, soulful, sparkling, spectacular, splendid, steady, successful, super(b), support(ing), supreme(ly)

L: laugh(ing), lavish, learn(ing), legendary, liberate(d), liberation, life, light, light-hearted, lively, living, love(able), loving, lucky, luminous, luxurious

U: ultimate, ultra, unconditionally, understanding, unique, unwavering, upbeat, uplifting, upstanding, useful

T: talent(ed), teacher, terrific, thankful, thriving, transcendent, transformative, triumphant, true, trusting, trustworthy, truth(ful)

Let's pick one word from each of the four lists associated with each letter of the word slut. Here is one combination:

S: Sincerely

L: Loving

U: Understanding

T: Trusting

Put it together so it flows: sincerely loving, understanding and trusting. So, if someone calls you or someone else a slut, you can tell them that it is not okay to insult people that way. You can tell yourself (and maybe the person expressing the word as an insult) that a different way to frame that word is as a **S**incerely **L**oving, **U**nderstanding and **T**rusting person.

Instead of the letter T representing the word trusting, we could use a phrase that is not on the list such as: towards self and others. Change the location of the word "and" and remove the comma so that it flows better: **S**incerely **L**oving and **U**nderstanding **T**owards self and others.

Here's another variation:

Sparkling

Liberation

Unconditionally

Triumphant!

Now it's your turn! Create a new acrostic if the word slut has been used against you, someone you care about, or a group with which you identify. (If not, please skip ahead to "Check in with your body.") Use the words on the lists above or fill in other words that are meaningful to you:

S: ....

L: ....

U: ....

T: ....

Check in with your body

Resmaa Menakem recommends the practice of noticing bodily sensations as part of the process of recognizing and healing racialized trauma.[9] Body-based awareness promotes resilience and acceptance of self and others.

Check in with your body to become conscious of how you experience various words. Take a few minutes to quietly pay attention to your breathing and body sensations. How are you feeling? What do you notice right now? Are you holding tension or feeling at ease? Where do you sense these feelings?

Imagine that someone walked up to you and called you a term that is hurtful. What do you notice about your breath and body now?[10]

Release that experience. Shake it off or dance it out if needed. Lie on the floor and feel your body supported by the floor or earth. Imagine yourself enjoying a taste of honey or another taste you love to soothe your system if needed. How is your breathing? Is your body feeling tense or relaxed now? Where do you feel it?

Next, imagine that someone walked up to you and said "sincerely loving, understanding and trusting" or a phrase that you created. How does your body and breath respond now?

Record any observations from this experience.

. . . .

. . . .

. . . .

Your turn to reframe it!

While the following words should not be used to describe yourself or others, they are, unfortunately, words that are commonly used. Consider one or more of these words for an acrostic you create. Circle the word you would like to reframe, or write in your own term.

Bad	Dirty	Loser
B*tch	Dumb	Ugly
Broke	Freak	Trash
Bum	Idiot	Weird
Crazy	Lazy	Whore/Ho

Write in: . . . .

Creating acrostics can be empowering and fun. Reclaim that power! If you are not sure how to come up with a set of affirming terms to choose from for a given letter, search online for a list of positive words. Let's use words that reflect care and dignity towards ourselves and others more often! Make it a conscious habit. It may even inspire others to do the same.

If you would prefer to create an acrostic using a different word or words, go for it! Caution: let's not attempt to reclaim or reframe slurs that do not affect us. Longer words are not included here but might include stupid, boring, illegal, cancelled, terrorist, savage, snowflake, worthless, train wreck, not enough, redneck, too much, unlovable and so on. Some words have been reclaimed for empowerment by the communities which were originally targeted by those words. For example, the word "dyke" can be a slur when directed in a hostile tone or it can be a word of power such as the title of the annual "Dyke March" for visibility and community among lesbians, queer, trans and non-binary people and allies. Even the word "queer" has a long history as a slur (and it may still be used harmfully). The word "fat" has been similarly reclaimed for empowerment by people in the body positivity movement. Fat can be a neutral way to describe a body. Other body-loving words include voluptuous, plump, curvy, Rubenesque, chunky, plump, thick, phat, plush(y), fluffy and lush.

Can you think of other words that have been reclaimed for empowerment?

. . . .

Here's some space for you to work out "Reframe it!" words of your choice:

Original word(s):

. . . .

What it represents:

. . . .

How can it be reframed for empowerment?

. . . .

. . . .

Write each letter of the word in a column. Record words with positive associations that start with those letters. If you need more space, please use your journal.

. . . .

. . . .

. . . .

. . . .

. . . .

. . . .

. . . .

Play around with various combinations of positive words until you are happy with the acrostic you create. Have fun with it!

Acrostic:

. . . .

. . . .

Who can you share this acrostic with?

....

/ ....

Great job using language as a tool of empowerment!

CHAPTER 3
KEEP MOTIVATED!

Let's learn what **motivates** Alise, Grayson, Helen and Soul to work towards personal and collective liberation and social justice.

Alise

I think the basis of being motivated and what keeps me grounded is thinking: I want to honor my mother and I want to honor those who are going to come after me. I just want people to have a good quality of life, one that isn't ridden by generational trauma or anxiety or just fear of being yourself. I think that the basis of a lot of social justice work is being compassionate towards yourself and others. Love and compassion are a really radical thing that people underestimate all the time. A big thing that just keeps me going is how frustrated I am with things. One big frustration that I have is that I know a lot of people who aren't really affected by the issues that I'm passionate about and they tell me just to be positive or work hard and get high up there so that I can change things. This contributes to that narrative that what's wrong with society is marginalized people's mindsets, not institutional deficits. A big part of my motivation is to try to be myself and to voice my concerns and to just be an unadulterated version of myself. That means taking time for myself, having self-care and not trying to change myself for others. That in itself is a form of activism. Ground yourself. See what type of activism works for you—because just preserving yourself, that's activism, too.

I really am motivated by art. I had been spending a lot of time on social media and seeing a lot about how Covid-19 is disproportionately affecting Black and Brown people. And it made me feel, "What can I do? I'm stuck at home?" So, when I notice myself getting kind of down, I try to look for more art. When you bring it back to the people, it feels so much more tangible. What motivates me most is being there for my friends and my family and being a good ally and making sure that they're the ones who are protected. And then by default, I'm someone who could be protected, too.

Grayson

One thing that motivates me is that I completely believe there can be a generation of youth, that I live to see, who will experience these things without even a question: introducing yourself with pronouns, switching pronouns when someone comes out, accepting people who express their gender in diverse ways, and so on. All of these things and more would have made life so much more bearable, even joyful, for me when I first came out.

One of my main motivators is trying to change society so that no one has to go through the same pain that I did. The hardest time in my life thus far was the months and even the few years following coming out as queer and trans to everyone I knew in my freshman year of high school. To live through that took a lot of strength. I could not be in school without being misgendered or called slurs, without people making transphobic jokes, threats or hate speech towards me. There were genuinely times when I didn't think that I would make it. We know how high the attempted suicide rate is for trans youth. [Note: An alarming and heartbreaking 52 percent of transgender and non-binary youth have seriously considered suicide in the last year and 41 percent have attempted suicide according to the

2020 Trevor Project Survey of over 40,000 LGBTQ youth aged 13–24 across the United States.[1]]

When I reached out to people to help alleviate the incessant transphobia I experienced, they always gave me, "I'm so sorry to hear that," but there was never any action behind those empty words, so I put action to the change I wanted to see. I had to find good in the world and look at all the people who are vocal about their love. Also, I had to find power in myself. That was a huge part of me healing. The moments where you realize that either you flipped your own life or you flipped someone else's life, those are the meaningful moments experienced by a changemaker. I am motivated to keep moving towards more of those moments.

Helen

I am partly motivated by my own experiences of marginalization and oppression that make me empathetic and sensitive to the impact of being marginalized and so I want to try and help the world become a place that is safer and not as cruel and painful as it has been at times for me because of homophobia and sexism. Also, it's just the right thing to try and do this work; using the position that I occupy socially and the skill set that I have to try and do that work is important. It just brings me joy. It's really fun for me. I like writing plays and I also really like doing sex education. I just enjoy educating others.

I've had depression all my life, and sometimes when I'm really depressed, my motivation dips, but generally I've been lucky to be a pretty ambitious, motivated person. When I have felt those motivation dips, like I needed inspiration, I look to the activism and art of those around me and that can be really compelling. There are also times when I feel really burned out or hopeless, and it's okay to take a break and watch a movie or something that's entirely disconnected from the world of activism. But even that kind of inspires me to get back into it, because really, all media say something about gender and sexuality and race and all these other identity politics, even if it is unintentional. It's just a part of being in society, that these identities influence us in a myriad of ways. I just want to stress for other people feeling burned out that it's okay to take breaks and to commiserate with others about how hard it can be to do this work. Take a bath, go for a walk, watch a show you love. You'll get inspired again.

Soul

Injustice. Injustice motivates me to work towards social justice. There's a quote, I believe from a rabbi, that's something along the lines of, "You are not required to finish the work, but neither are you free to abandon it."[2] I feel that in my soul. I know that I have the power to change things. And I think that is a motivation as well, knowing that I'm capable and that I can use my privilege to do things. Being financially secure has privileged me  in all these different ways. So, yes, injustice affects me. Bullying really affected me. In special education, I was still traumatized by that. But because of my family's financial security, there is so much that I've been able to skate by with. Like when I came out as non-binary and they didn't really understand. There was a support group for parents that they had access to, not just because they could afford to send me to the pediatric hospital's gender clinic but also because they could afford to take time off work to go to these things. There was still a time where I felt unsupported and things were difficult, but it was such a short amount of time. I look at the other trans people and non-binary people in my life and their families are so difficult. Of course, they still love them and all that, but I dodged that because my community offered these resources (the gender clinic, the Trans Wellness Conference, the support groups) and my parents and I had the opportunity to utilize them.

We live in strange times now, and I can tell you, I've been motivated to make art and just share myself and share my energy and celebrate those things. Talking with my family about the work I'm doing is motivating. I do have depression and other underlying issues and sometimes that makes it pretty impossible. And I say to myself, "This is okay. I need to take care of myself right now. Trees don't produce fruit in every season." You know?

And sometimes we do just have off days. And I also remind myself that not only is every day or every hour a fresh start, but so is every minute. I can listen to myself and wait until the answer is yes again without expectation. So, do the work. Show up when you can. Keep working when you're still energized and inspired. So now I set a timer for ten minutes and I go through and I do the work and I get it done. And when the timer goes off, I'm like, "Okay, time to do something else." And I'm still feeling good. I'm still in the zone, you know? Stop when you're still feeling energized. Don't burn off all that energy on this project. Have several things you can cycle through. It's been like a miracle for me.

Reflection: What motivates you to make a difference?

What intrigues you about what Alise, Grayson, Helen and Soul shared about their motivations? What motivates you to make a difference?

. . . .

. . . .

. . . .

Alise emphasizes love and compassion and shares that she wants "people to have a good quality of life; one that isn't ridden by generational trauma or anxiety or just fear of being yourself." Is that something you want? Is that something you can be in service towards?

. . . .

. . . .

. . . .

Have you had any experiences such as what Grayson describes as "the moments where you realize that either you flipped your own life or you flipped someone else's life"? Do you think of yourself as a changemaker as Grayson does?

. . . .

. . . .

. . . .

Grayson shares, "look at all the people who are vocal about their love" and find power in yourself as healing. What are your strategies for moving through challenges or staying motivated?

. . . .

. . . .

. . . .

In her memoir *We Are Not Here to Be Bystanders* (2020), Linda Sarsour, Palestinian American Muslim community organizer and National Co-chair of the 2017 Women's March, echoes Grayson's sentiments. She writes, "In an age of alternative facts, fake news, and emboldened racism and xenophobia, we cannot be silent. We cannot allow the voices of hate and divisiveness to be louder than the voices of solidarity and love."[3]

How are you using your voice for solidarity and love? If you are not yet doing so, how could you show solidarity and love?

. . . .

. . . .

. . . .

Soul says, "I have the power to change things. And I think that is a motivation as well, knowing that I'm capable and that I can use my privilege to do things." Helen describes "using the position that I occupy socially and the skill set that I have" to make a difference. What privilege and social positions do you have? Let's think about that further in our next activity.

Gratitude

Let's consider things that we hold dear in our lives and things that we might want to change. In her book *Braiding Sweetgrass: Indigenous Wisdom, Scientific Knowledge and the Teachings of Plants* (2013), botanist, professor and Citizen Potawatomi Nation member Robin Wall Kimmerer, Ph.D., shares the Onondaga-language "Words That Come Before All Else"[4] expression of gratitude to all relations (including animals, insects, plants and earth) as a process of honoring our reciprocal relationships and connecting human minds and spirits.

What are three things you are grateful for?

1. ....

2. ....

3. ....

Are your gratitude items things you think that other people might be grateful for, too? Are these things that others might take for granted or assume that they are just "givens" or expected?

....

....

....

What are three things you would change about the world if you could?

1. ....

2. ....

3. ....

Are your world change items things that others might also want to change? Are these things that others might consider inevitable or obstacles?

....

....

Check your privilege

The next activity is intended to help organize your thinking about advantages and marginalization you might experience based on society's constructed favoritism. Only major categories are described in the chart. If you have ideas about other important advantages or disadvantages at play in your life, please write them on the blank rows at the end of the chart.

Why do we want to consider our privilege anyway? Isn't it just going to make us feel bad to know that we have it better or worse than other people/groups? Well, it depends. The intention of the activity is not to make you feel bad. It is to help you recognize the forces and systems that are at play in all of our lives so we can leverage our privilege in service of the greater good whenever possible.

Please keep in mind that even people with relative privilege may still experience hardships, injustice and trauma. Privilege does not always protect us from challenging life experiences. Yet, people with relative privilege are often less likely to experience hardships, injustice and trauma than marginalized people. For example, white people are not likely to have endured the kinds of racialized traumas that are, unfortunately, everyday indignities for BIPOC.

Please read across each line in the following chart. Decide if you have a relative advantage or are marginalized for each item. Put a check mark (✓) in the box that best describes your experience. If you are not sure or if it's complicated, feel free to skip the item or put check marks in both boxes.

✓	Relative advantage (privilege)	✓	Marginalized (in U.S. society currently)
	I am white or white-passing.		I am Black, Indigenous, a person of color or a person of multiple races/ cultures.
	I am a man/boy.		I am a woman/girl.
	I am cisgender (identifying with the gender assigned to me at birth) and generally fit within society's expectations for my gender presentation (style, mannerisms, voice).		I am transgender, non-binary, genderqueer, gender nonconforming, gender expansive, gender creative or another of the infinitely diverse genders.
	I am straight.		I am queer, lesbian, gay, bisexual, pansexual, asexual or another sexual orientation.
	I do not have a physical disability.		I have a physical disability.
	I am neurotypical (not neurodiverse).		I am neurodiverse (autistic, dyslexic, have ADHD, OCD or dyscalculia).
	I am an age that is considered neither "too young" nor "too old."		I am considered "too young" or "too old."
	I have a typical body size.		I have a body size that is larger or smaller than what is considered typical.
	My family's religion is the predominant religion in my country (in the U.S. = Christianity).		My family's religion is Muslim, Jewish, Buddhist, Hindu, Sikh, pagan, another religion, or atheist.
	I do not have mental/behavioral health issues.		I have mental/behavioral health issues.

cont.

✓	Relative advantage (privilege)	✓	Marginalized (in U.S. society currently)
	I do not have an ongoing health issue.		I have an ongoing health issue.
	I have not been incarcerated, nor has someone I care about.		I have been incarcerated and/or someone I care about has been incarcerated.
	My family owns property.		My family does not own property.
	My family has had consistent income that is enough to meet our needs.		My family's income has not been consistently enough to meet our needs.
	My family has inherited wealth (money, property).		My family has not inherited wealth (money, property).
	One or more people in my family have gone to college.		My family has not been college-educated.
	I have had secure housing throughout my life.		I have experienced housing insecurity.
	I have had food security throughout my life.		I have experienced food insecurity.
	I have consistent access to safe drinking water.		I have not always had access to safe drinking water.
	I am a citizen.		I am not a citizen or not yet a citizen.
	I speak fluent mainstream English without an accent.		I speak an English dialect or have an accent.
	I don't have to think about my identities. The world works for me.		I think about how I am perceived and behave in certain ways in an effort to keep myself safe.
	I am being/was educated in a well-funded school or setting.		I am being/was educated in an underinvested school or setting.
	My neighborhood/community is well funded.		My neighborhood/community is underinvested.
	Write in:		Write in:
	Write in:		Write in:

How did that activity go for you? What are some of the areas where you might leverage your privilege? How might you do that?

. . . .

. . . .

. . . .

Can you imagine?

What if the first ten (or all!) advantages on the "Check your privilege" chart were considered marginalized and vice versa? Does this sound scary or exciting? What would be different in society? How might you walk through the world differently? What concerns might you have that you don't have now? What concerns could you release that you or loved ones have been carrying?

. . . .

. . . .

. . . .

Great job engaging with what is sometimes considered challenging content! If you would like to continue thinking deeply about how privilege operates for various identities, there are many useful checklists online. You could also create your own list. Just ask yourself in every interaction: how am I privileged or not in this moment and based on which identity? How does privilege operate in this situation/system?

Next time you hear the expression "check your privilege," pause, breathe and recall this activity. Remember that privilege is designed to keep people unaware of the systemic benefits they hold and the ways individuals, groups and communities are harmed by being marginalized. Keep listening and learning from people with lived experience of marginalization so we can work towards justice and equity.

Chill break or shake it out!

Let's pause for a minute to pay attention to how you are feeling in your body. Do you notice any sensations? If you'd like to chill out, that's great. Mindfully notice your breathing and energy for the next 60 seconds. If you'd like a movement energizer, please stretch in ways that feel good to your body. Shake out your hands, feet and whole body if you are able and willing to do so. Enliven yourself!

Accepting yourself and others

Here are four options for you to consider. Check the one that generally applies to you (✓).

- ❏   1. I feel most comfortable with people who are like me
- ❏   2. I feel most comfortable with people who are different from me
- ❏   3. I am open to all people
- ❏   4. I am willing to work through any discomfort to connect with people who have different life experiences from mine

Now, let's dive a little deeper into each of those statements. Please respond to the follow-up questions about the item number you selected above.

1. In what ways are other people like you? What makes you feel comfortable about that similarity?

   ....

2. In what ways are other people different from you? What makes you feel comfortable about that difference?

   ....

3. How diverse is your friend group? How are they diverse?

....

4. How do you connect with people of different life experiences?

....

Can you accept and appreciate your own unique set of experiences, features and identities? What is one thing you can do to honor yourself even more?

....

....

....

What is one belief/story/generalization you hold about people who share a common identity with you?

....

....

....

What is the origin of this idea?

....

....

....

What is one belief/story/generalization you hold about people who do not share this same identity?

. . . .

. . . .

. . . .

What is the origin of this idea?

. . . .

. . . .

. . . .

Are those beliefs/stories/generalizations serving you? How?

. . . .

. . . .

. . . .

If the stories are not serving you regarding people who share and/or do not share a common identity with you, write a new story that focuses on dignity and respect.

. . . .

. . . .

. . . .

Flip the script!

We have been socially conditioned to like or dislike certain things and believe certain things without even realizing it. How does this happen? Through the images we see (or an absence of positive, inclusive representations) on television and the movies, through social media, through advertising, laws, policies and practices and through the behavior of people around us, we pick up on things we were probably not formally taught.

The statements below are intended to help us "flip the script" to recognize imbalances that we may have been conditioned to believe, often unconsciously. The statements should not be used to stereotype, make anyone an object or put them on a pedestal. There are differences among members of any group. Avoid generalizations. They are used in this activity to challenge assumptions. Always recognize the humanity, dignity and complexity of all people.

If you find yourself having a strong reaction to any of the statements below, that might be an indication that there are harmful social messages programmed beyond your conscious awareness. Take a moment to mindfully slow down. Pause, breathe and feel into your body. We'll explore items that invoke strong reactions after the list.

Put a plus sign (+) in the box if you agree with the statement. Put a minus sign (–) if you disagree with the statement. Put a circle around the box if you have a strong reaction to the statement.

❏ Women are strong and smart

❏ "Real" men and boys cry and express their vulnerabilities

❏ People living in poverty are hardworking and resourceful

❏ People with disabilities are highly qualified and have many skills

❏ Darker skin tones are gorgeous

❏ Fat bodies are beautiful

❏ Queerness is fabulous

❏ All gender identities and gender expressions are marvelous and valid

❏ Black and Latinx men are virtuous and have multiple intelligences

❏ Neurodiverse people see and experience the world in important ways

❏ Indigenous peoples are revitalizing traditional practices

❏ Asian/Pacific Islander Americans and Latinx Americans are citizens who have been in the U.S. for generations

❏ People with mental/behavioral health issues are resilient

❏ Muslims are peaceful

❏ Jewish people are generous

❏ Young people are wise

What are some other important statements to help recognize or neutralize harmful social programming? Write down your ideas:

. . . .

. . . .

. . . .

Be a brave investigator!

For items you circled and had a strong reaction to, ask yourself, where did that reaction come from? Does it serve me? Who does it serve?

If you argued with the statement and refused to accept it, what was the message that came through? For example, if you read, "People living in poverty are hardworking and resourceful" and heard yourself say, "If they were hardworking, they wouldn't be living in poverty," ask yourself: What evidence do I have that it is true? What impact does that message have on people from that group? Does it dehumanize? Does it take into account people who are working multiple jobs with low wages and no sick leave or medical insurance? Does it consider inequitable policies which create disadvantage for groups of people?

The statements may hold a charge because we have been conditioned by patriarchy, white supremacy (including white beauty standards), the gender binary, other harmful systems and capitalism to buy into (literally, to buy and consume!) assumptions and expectations about groups of people. When we become conscious about those beliefs, we can see systems that perpetuate harm in action and even alive within us. Dr. Ibram X. Kendi urges us to remember that behavior can only be attributed to the individual, not the race (or other social identity) and that all cultures have equal value; none is superior or inferior.[5]

In *Biased: Uncovering the Hidden Prejudice that Shapes What We See, Think and Do*, social psychology researcher and professor Jennifer L. Eberhardt, Ph.D., describes how bias "conditions how we look at the world and the people within it, despite our conscious motivations and desires" and that we are "conditioned by racial narratives that narrow our vision and bias how we see the people around us."[6] Can we work towards making our biases conscious every day?

If you find yourself having a strong reaction, pause and ask yourself where that thought/argument/refusal to accept might have come from. Here are a few options. Check all that apply (✓):

- ❏ Is it based on your personal experience?

- ❏ Did someone in a position of authority voice this sentiment? Who? (Refer back to the "Judging or criticizing" list in Chapter 1 if needed.) ....

- ❏ Is this something you heard or saw in the media?

- ❏ Is it based on the lack of representation (invisibility/omission)?

- ❏ Is it based on social structures (such as gendered restrooms or segregated schools or neighborhoods)?

❏   Is it the way that people respond about this subject or around this group?

❏   Write in: ....

Now, use your favorite strategy from "The shame and stigma shut down" activity in Chapter 1 to neutralize the harmful social programming.

Ultimately, let us remember that people are complex and multifaceted beings. There is no one aspect that defines a person's entire existence. We can all learn from each other, support each other, recognize our interdependence and work together to change inequitable policies and practices and create equitable and inclusive cultures.

CHAPTER 4
TRANSFORMATION, LIBERATION AND RAINBOWS!

This chapter features experiences of transformation and liberation on a personal and social level. One project which is an awesome model for social transformation is the Rainbow Dance. As president of his school's Gender and Sexuality Alliance (GSA), Grayson and GSA co-presidents and members led the school in creating a more welcoming and accepting school culture.

Model project: The Rainbow Dance

The Rainbow Dance is a sanctuary space for LGBTQ+ high school students and allies. It is a great beacon of hope and joy and a beautiful project which can be used as a model for your school or community to help create a more welcoming and accepting school/community culture. The Rainbow Dance includes students of all identities/demographics.

Now, let's enjoy Grayson's reflections about this project!

Grayson
The Rainbow Dance has been, honestly, one of the best things that I've done in this life so far. The Rainbow Dance creates a space where LGBTQ+ people can feel safe slow dancing with their partner, and able to

Welcome to the Rainbow Dance!

celebrate who they are and express themselves in the ways that they may not feel safe expressing themselves at homecoming, or prom, or any predominantly cisgender or straight space, for that matter. This event was created to foster support and make people in our community feel safe, loved and celebrated.

About 90 people came to the first dance, and the second year it was 150. The next year we broke 200! I really hope to keep that growing, making it bigger and better and being able to raise more money for an LGBTQ+ center for unhoused youth. We've developed fundraisers throughout the year that we use to pay off the actual cost of the dance so that all of the ticket proceeds go straight to the organization itself. I think that the fundraisers also are an amazing way to bring the LGBTQ+ community and our work into the school community and the local community.

It is a year-long effort, but that night makes it so worthwhile. It is one of the most beautiful things I've ever seen. I've watched it grow and become not only GSA members and their friends, but really the entire school community coming together and celebrating LGBTQ+ identities, their peers who are in that community, and giving back to the community as a whole.

My favorite part of it is to see the people filter in and I love seeing the way that people express themselves differently from how they do in other spaces and at other events. I see male-identifying people painting their nails and wearing brightly colored clothes which—they have told me personally—they would never do in any other space. And people wearing sequined dresses and suits, you know, whatever it may be. I just love the way that people feel safe expressing themselves. It adds to the idea that, for me personally, I know I've helped to create a safe space for people. It's sad that people can't dress that way whenever they want—because they feel like they can't—but the Rainbow Dance creates a space where they can. And even I wore makeup to the last Rainbow Dance, which was pretty fun because I know that there's no judgment. People are just there to have fun and celebrate who they are. I just love that.

I also love it when people talk to me, as one of the leaders of the Rainbow Dance, and tell me it's their favorite event of the year, and how it makes them feel so safe, and how they went home and they journaled about it or they had a good crying session—you know, a happy crying session—about it. Knowing that it has such a powerful effect on people's lives is so important to me. Everyone has the power to create change, and knowing that is very empowering—empowering and liberating.

I hope it will be a long-standing tradition at school and inspire other schools to follow in our footsteps. I want to change the world but we're starting on a small scale [laughs].

Reflection questions: Affirming spaces

Have you ever been in a space that was fun, affirming and in which you felt safe to express yourself fully? What was that like? When and where did it happen? Who created it? Is it ongoing? Has it yet to happen for you? Can you imagine what it might look like, sound like and feel like to be in such a space?

. . . .

. . . .

. . . .

What stands out to you most about Grayson's reflection on the Rainbow Dance?

. . . .

. . . .

. . . .

Extending the Rainbow Dance!

Could you envision a Rainbow Dance at your school or in your community? Would you be willing to contribute your energy to make that happen? Who could you invite to collaborate with you? (We'll explore crafting a project more fully in Chapter 10.)

. . . .

. . . .

. . . .

Now, let's hear from Alise, Grayson, Helen and Soul about their experiences with **transformation and liberation** and if they feel responsibility and urgency in their efforts.

Alise

I experienced transformation in the 2019 summer program that I went to. The space was oriented towards marginalized people: people of color, queer people and gender nonconforming people. The demographics were just completely different from what I was used to, which was refreshing. People were much more self-aware and intuitive and much more careful with other people's feelings than I experienced at school. The community was super adaptive and focused on making everyone included and catering to everyone's needs. There was a "call-in" culture, which means correcting someone with love and respect instead of employing the public humiliation that often comes with calling out. So, if you saw something or someone said something to you that hurt you, you could call them in and there was just a community of receptiveness that I'd never had before. If you call someone in at high school, they're just like, "Oh my gosh, you're insulting me." But at the summer program it was, "Thank you for educating me" and they'd realize that it was not some tragic flaw, but something that they could change.

There was a really weird gender dynamic for the first two weeks of the summer program where there were five guys and they just dominated the space even though there were 15 of us in total. So, we ended up having a call-in session. It was very raw and super real. After that we had to talk about further steps. That was a big moment for me because I'd voiced some of my concerns and I was worried I was not going to have my running buddies anymore. These were my bros. These were the people who I really loved. If I told them that they'd hurt me, was I going to lose them? But they were super receptive to our concerns. There was the realization for me that relationships should be receptive, they should be reciprocal and much more adaptive than they have been in the past for me. And that was a big moment. Now I feel much more comfortable voicing my concerns and I know what to look for in friendships. Allyship should be part of friendship. They should not be two separate things. That was a big realization for me that I still hold on to.

Grayson

All of the moments when I realized that my fight had got me somewhere, those are the best and most transformational moments. I was Homecoming King this year. People supported me and they cheered for me. People were happy when I won. You know, thinking that I used to be the kid who hid under the staircase during lunch because I was too afraid to go to the lunch room, and then winning Homecoming King three years  later, it's a very 180 moment. There was a very long time in my life where I never even thought I would be able to come out. I never thought I would be accepted. I never thought I would have that support. Seeing the community that has surrounded me has been amazing. It's bigger than me. I didn't just win as another kid, I won as a trans man, and that is powerful. I started high school as someone who people didn't even acknowledge as a man and now I'm leaving it as King [laughs]. I don't even know how to put it into words, but the support that I felt is truly extraordinary. I wish that for anyone who had to go through the hardships I did. When I first came out, that moment of liberation, of "okay, I'm finally free to be myself," was stolen from me by all of the abandonment, harassment and pain that I went through as a product of simply being myself. That is what makes these moments so meaningful to me. Other moments that stand out in my mind are seeing my chest for the first time after top surgery, getting elected to the student council, giving my biggest speeches, and winning awards for my activism. The one thing that all these moments have in common is that they are evidence of my growth and all I have overcome. When you have struggled as much as I have with acceptance and tolerance and finding your place in the world, these small moments of joy become a lot more victorious. The moments where you feel that you can be yourself are the most beautiful of all. This is exactly why I continue to fight for my community. We all deserve the opportunity to feel this way.

Helen

A big transformation for me was when I started taking college-level gender theory classes and was exposed to big ideas like "gender is a social construct." These ideas really shook my world and made me reconsider my own identities. I stopped being so tied to the "woman" identity and, while that's a label that is sometimes useful to me, such as when I'm talking about instances of sexism I have faced, it's not something that I feel is a core part of my being the way it is for some people I know. I've found that I'm really connected to femininity and really like the "femme" identity, but that's about gender expression, about my affect and interests and the way I express myself. Anyone can be femme, regardless of body or of gender identity. That was a breakthrough for me, realizing that I can be femme and that doesn't make me a traitor to feminism or necessarily mean I'm a woman. I've embraced this femme identity in a way that lets me hold space for people who aren't usually femme (butch women and masculine man friends) but who can be femme with me. I think that's especially important for trans men or genderqueer people who were assigned female at birth and who usually occupy a more masculine space but might sometimes want to do femme things without having their identities questioned or feel like they're not "doing trans right."

Sexual violence is a problem in college and everywhere. So, it's important to try and have conversations about consent and desire openly, ideally in ways that are non-aggressive or combative. I really do believe in rehabilitation and rehabilitative models of making the world better. I don't think that just because someone's done something reprehensible we should leave them and say goodbye, or ostracize them. But I also think something must be done. Whose job is it to educate? I can try to talk to people, at parties or whatever, and encourage them to seek treatment in therapy. But it's especially difficult to encourage people who you're not close to. A lot of people don't like hearing that they need to see a therapist from random feminists at parties.

Soul

One specific thing I think of as a moment of liberation is removing that gender/sex checkbox on my university application that you, Sherry, helped me with, and that was really devastating to me, kind of out of the blue. What was really amazing to me was that by the time I got to the Glass Department, it was completely a matter of course to introduce ourselves with name and pronouns.

There's always more work to do. It's little thing after little thing after little thing where I can look back after years and be like, "Wow, things have changed." I don't feel urgency. I just have to be out here doing my small bit; you know, put on your oxygen mask before you help your neighbor. There's a quote that's something to the effect of, if all you did was make a garden, you made the world a better place.[1]

Reflection: What experiences have you had with transformation and liberation?

What do you most appreciate about what Alise, Grayson, Helen and Soul shared about their experiences with transformation and liberation? What experiences have you had with transformation and liberation?

. . . .

. . . .

. . . .

Alise talks about a "call-in culture" of receptiveness towards recognizing and taking responsibility for something that was said or done which was hurtful. Have you experienced such a culture? Can you imagine what that might look like, sound like and feel like? How can we work towards creating cultures in our homes, schools, workplaces and communities in which we can care for each other as we educate each other, acknowledge harm and work towards repairing that harm?

. . . .

. . . .

. . . .

Grayson shares his perspective: "The moments where you feel like you can be yourself are the most beautiful in the world." Do you agree? Have you had such an experience? What was that like?

. . . .

. . . .

. . . .

My/Our transformation, liberation and healing

The next few prompts are about the personal level. They could also be considered on a collective level (read "you" as "we" and "your" as "our"). If you are working with a group, have each person respond individually, listen to each person's response and then collaborate to create a shared statement for each prompt.

What do you need to be liberated from? What are you healing from?

. . . .

. . . .

. . . .

What is your liberation towards? What are you working towards?

. . . .

. . . .

. . . .

What do you want to see transformed?

. . . .

. . . .

. . . .

Creativity time!

Write a poem, story or song with any or all of the following words or create a visual work of art or dance inspired by one or more of the words. Feel free to add your own big ideas to this list:

Acceptance	Harm	Sanctuary
Action	Healing	Shame
Adversity	Humanity	Silencing
Allies/collaborators/ accomplices	Injustice	Society
	Inspiration	Speaking out
Care	Invisibility	Stigma
Collective	Justice	Transformation
Community	Liberation	Trauma
Diversity	Oppression	Visibility
Empower	Power	We
Freedom	Respite/rest	World
Grieving	Restoration	. . . .

....

....

....

....

....

....

....

....

....

....

....

Let's play!

Author, speaker and intuitive practitioner Melissa Joy Jonsson describes PLAY as "**P**otential **L**ove **A**waiting **Y**ou."[2] How beautiful! Let's find the fun in big and small ways in our lives. In honor of legendary drag queen RuPaul Charles, can we imagine dancing or "sashaying down the runway" of hallways, supermarket aisles and sidewalks? Can we frolic more? Skip? Jump? Can we sing out loud and move with joy? Play hand-clapping games? Color? Thumb wrestle? Can we make up our own little games with our friends (in person or virtual)? Make up songs and stories? Have dance parties? Laugh more? Do you have a positive response to the words "Go play outside"? How can you tap into the energy of play more?

. . . .

. . . .

. . . .

Now, put that PLAY into action! Can you "find the fun" three times a day?

Let's PLAY with the colors of the rainbow in honor of the Rainbow Dance!

The rainbow ray within!

This is an invitation to play with the colors of the rainbow through imagery and movement. Please take it at your own pace and adapt this activity to suit your needs. Perhaps you prefer to draw or paint with the colors. Perhaps you want to gather objects of each color and hold them in your hand. Perhaps you want to move only with one color or only with the full rainbow and not individual colors. Perhaps you want to sing or hum the vibration of the color instead of move with it. That's AWESOME! Do whatever feels best to you. You are also welcome to experience the colors while sitting or lying down in stillness.

Directions:

1. Read through each of the color descriptions below. For reference, naturally occurring elements of each color are listed such as fruits, vegetables, animals and crystals/minerals. This is not an exhaustive list. If you love an object that is a certain color but it is not listed here, such as an orange basketball or yellow tennis ball, your favorite purple sneakers or your animal companion, write that in on the blank line. Circle your favorite item(s) or your "write in" item from each color category and call that to mind as we play with and experience each color.
2. Read the prompts which are included as a script at the end of this activity to connect with the experience of each color. For example, perhaps you are working with the color red and you chose beets. Beets are a root vegetable, so maybe you feel their energy in the ground and that activates the energy in your feet. Let the energy of the beet red vibrate in your feet and upwards throughout your whole body. How does that energy/vibration feel?
3. You may want to create an audio recording of your voice reminding you of your favorite items and the prompts so that you can just relax into the experience. Feel free to put on your favorite music in the background.
4. Continue experimenting with the other colors. Where do you feel each one? How does it move you? Does a blue jay eating a blueberry with a clear blue sky in the background give you an expansive feeling? Let your imagination create awesome combinations. Play!

As we are working with the more inclusive "Philadelphia Rainbow Flag" as a reference, let's start with the colors black and brown. Note: The color indigo is found in the rainbow but it is not listed here. Please feel free to add indigo or any other color that you would like to work with.

Black: black rice, blackberries, black licorice, black garlic, black beans, black pepper, black lentils, squid ink, black sesame seeds, charcoal, crow, panther, black tourmaline, black onyx, obsidian, smoky quartz, the night sky (unless there is light pollution or aurora borealis), space

Write in: . . . .

Brown: maple syrup, molasses, tea, cacao beans, pinto beans, brown lentils, cinnamon, vanilla bean, coffee, chocolate, honey, caramel, potato, peanut, almond, soil, clay, wood, tree bark, coconut shell, bear, camel, deer, monkey, tiger's eye gemstone

Write in: . . . .

Red: red apple, red rose, watermelon, strawberry, tomato, cherry, raspberries, red pepper (sweet or hot), pomegranate, red radish, the red cardinal bird, garnet gemstone

Write in: . . . .

Orange: tangerine, orange, clementine, carrot, sweet potato, yam, butternut squash, pumpkin, cantaloupe, mango, peach, nectarine, persimmon, apricot, papaya, acorn squash, turmeric, marigold flowers, orange zinnias, orange day lilies, monarch butterfly, orangutan, orange fish (koi, goldfish, clownfish), the ancient resin amber

Write in: . . . .

Yellow: banana, lemon, pineapple, yellow bell pepper, corn, star fruit, golden apple, yellow pear, yellow summer squash, spaghetti squash, ginger, sunflowers, daffodils, yellow day lilies, yellow duckling, yellow birds (goldfinch, warbler), yellow fish (butterflyfish, electric yellow fish, yellow tang), citrine crystal

Write in: . . . .

Green: broccoli, asparagus, brussels sprouts, celery, kale, cucumber, lettuce, avocado, zucchini, jalapeño, artichoke, green apple, green grapes, green pear, lime, kiwi, peas, herbs, pistachios, leaves, grass, many frogs and lizards and snakes, green parrots, the gemstone jade

Write in: ....

Blue: blue corn, blueberries, sky, ocean, blue butterfly, blue jay bird, peacock's body, delphiniums, hydrangea, blue iris flowers, bluebell flowers, blue jeans (indigo dye), blue fish (blue betta fish, royal blue tang, blue damselfish), lapis lazuli, turquoise

Write in: ....

Purple: grapes, plums, lavender flowers, eggplant, elderberries, figs, purple asparagus, purple cabbage, purple carrots, purple potatoes, allium flowers, purple iris flowers, purple crocuses, purple calla lilies, purple fish (purple betta fish, purple dottyback), amethyst crystals

Write in: ....

Other color you would like to add: ....

Write in one or more items which are the color you are adding:

....

Script

Notice your breath. Pay attention to how you feel right now and before you begin this "Rainbow ray within" color play experience.

Tune into the color .... Imagine or hold a .... (color) .... (name one or more items you selected). See/hear/feel/smell/taste/touch/ sense/experience the .... 's (color/item) attributes such as texture, weight or size. Feel the vibration of the color .... in your body. Where do you feel it? Let the energy of the color

. . . . *flow throughout your body. If you like, move with that energy/vibration. Match its vibration with your movement. Is that vibration fast or slow? Does it have a temperature or texture? How does that vibration feel? Let it move you in unexpected (and safe) ways. Express it as a sound/hum/tone if you would like.*

Repeat the paragraph above as many times as needed for each of the colors you want to include.

Finally, include the rainbow or whatever combination of colors you would like to bring together.

Script continued
Now, let's bring in all the colors of the rainbow in and around you. Express the rainbow through movement or sound or just feel the energy/vibration. Frolic, hum, fully express yourself! See/hear/feel/smell/taste/touch/sense/ experience the rainbow all around you and through your body. Take as much time as you want here.

Options for ending

1. **Wrap up** here and come back into the present moment. **Ending script:** *Now, let's begin the journey back. Gently bring your awareness back to your body and the room/place where you are located. Notice your breath. Become aware of your position. Feel your feet on the ground or imagine sending your roots into the Earth. Take your time becoming fully present. Come back to the moment with gratitude for your experience.*
2. **Extend the rainbow to a wider location:** If you would like to try expanding the rainbow, continue with the "Extension" prompts below.
3. **Fall asleep:** If you would like to use this as a way to help you fall asleep, just allow yourself to relax deeply into the vibration of the color(s).

Extension

[Note: If you prefer to use a single color or set of colors of your choice, just substitute that color or set of colors for the word "rainbow" in this script.]

Extension script: If you would like to explore extending the rainbow beyond your body, enjoy the journey!

Let's extend the rainbow beyond our bodies. See the rainbow effortlessly encompassing your home, your neighborhood/town/community, including all the natural elements, life forms and people. See it continuing beyond the immediate vicinity to drift into neighboring communities. Allow the rainbow to shimmer throughout your country, to the continent, to all continents and islands of the globe. See the rainbow flowing within and through the oceans and skies. See it dancing over every surface of the Earth and permeating deeply into the Earth. Trust that the energy of the rainbow flows as needed. To complete our rainbow play, see the Earth as a sphere with a rainbow around and through it. Just allow it to float gently in space. Give it your love and gratitude.

At this point, you can choose to wrap up (read the words from the **Wrap up** above) or fall asleep.

   Notice how you feel after you have completed the activity.

   Take some time to relax after the color play experience. Use the space in the following pages to draw/paint/collage and/or to journal about your experience.

   Come back to this "Rainbow ray within" experience as often as you like. Experiment with other colors or use the same colors every time and see if there are any changes in your experience. Notice and honor the colors everywhere in nature and in your everyday life.

Rainbow ray within drawing/painting/collage-creating space

Use this space to express what came through for you during your color play experience.

Rainbow ray within journal

In the color play experience, I felt/noticed:

. . . .

. . . .

. . . .

How does this experience relate to diversity? Does it help you appreciate natural and human diversity?

. . . .

. . . .

. . . .

The "Rainbow ray within" options for daily practice

Five minutes a day

Take five minutes a day to explore a single color for the week. For example, start week 1 with the color black. Here are some prompts to consider: How have we been conditioned to fear the dark or regard it less favorably than the light? How do we reclaim the dark? Can we get to know its power, presence and peace? Can you feel into the spaciousness, the expansion, the infinite? If you find yourself having strong feelings or reactions to any color, pause and write about it. What thoughts do you notice? What stories are associated with it? Where do those stories come from? Do you want to look away or not engage with a particular color? Why might that be? Talk to a friend, family member or trusted support person about your thoughts, feelings, concerns and hopes. It might be useful to find a partner who is willing to share their experiences with you and check in with each other. A collaborative exploration can really enrich the experience. Consider working with a group if that option is available!

. . . .

. . . .

. . . .

For week 2, play with the color brown for five minutes a day. Ask yourself the same questions as above.

Continue exploring each rainbow color for five minutes a day for the following weeks. Experiment with other colors of your choice.

Fifteen to twenty minutes a day
Allow yourself to experience the full "Rainbow ray within" color play for 15–20 minutes per day. This could be done early in the morning, just before bed, on a lunch break or at your convenience. Make it work for your schedule. Allow it to become a practice that you can access and go to in times of challenge and in quiet moments.

Black and brown stripes

Why is it important that we include the colors black and brown in the rainbow flag? How have BIPOC been marginalized in the LGBTQ+ Pride and Rights Movement? Whose voices and experiences are centered? Whose life is represented? Who is visible or invisible in the media? In our minds?

. . . .

. . . .

. . . .

Can you name some famous BIPOC, LGBTQ+ and/or Two Spirit people? Do some research online. Find a new role model!

CHAPTER 5
SUPPORT SYSTEMS AND ALLYSHIP

Some essential aspects of sustaining efforts to make a difference include building a support system and having allies who take action. We'll hear from Alise, Grayson, Helen and Soul about their experiences in building support systems. Later in the chapter, we'll get their thoughts about how allies can help make a difference.

How do you **build support systems** so you don't have to go it alone?

Alise

I find support systems in summer programs and different art opportunities that I've had. Young Playwrights is super activism-focused and they elevate important and diverse stories that need to be heard, which I appreciate. So, artistic spaces and spaces where I can be myself, have fun and smile are really important to me in finding support. That's super important, just having people that you can really be yourself with. Even if it's just virtually, I have people who I've met over the summer who have a really special place in my heart.

Grayson

I don't think there's just one way to build a support system. It's different for everyone. For me, I started finding a bunch of people through my everyday endeavors who I consider to be safe people. And from there I built a group of people who I felt I could go to when, at the end of the day, I was so down that I didn't know what to do. I'm so lucky and so grateful to have found my group of people now who I can confide in and who, some of them, can relate to some of the struggles that I go through. Having designated LGBTQ+ spaces, like the GSA or whatever it may be outside schools, is so important. There are things out there, places out there, that you can go to and find people who are like you. It's so important to be around people who understand you. And for LGBTQ+ people, that's not always the easiest thing. It's scary seeking that sometimes because you don't know who's accepting and who's not. The incoming freshmen who I have had such a privilege to meet through GSA give me so much hope for the future. Seeing people advocating and fighting and being out, loud and proud of who they are is just so liberating and freeing.

Helen

I have definitely made friends here in college, but not the deep level of friendship that I have with my squad back home. I think a lot of that is the fact that we all sort of trained each other to be really good friends. A lot of people I've met have lower expectations from their friends than I do. They seek out a lower level of intimacy and support than the enormous affection and love and intimacy that I have with my friends back home. I think more love is good. And I'm happy to take love wherever it comes—partnerships as well as friends and anyone else. I don't think that having a support network with only one person, and that person is your intimate partner, is a sustainable way of living.

Soul

Being in a supportive art environment and being so well accommodated has made neurodiversity a non-issue in my life. I had a lot of difficulty with it in high school. I feel completely supported now. I've read some books and memoirs from other people who are neurodiverse and that has helped me. That's really given me a sense of belonging and community. And in the current communities I've been in, it's been a lot easier to connect with people. I do a lot of activism writing non-fiction. I collaborate with randos on the internet who want a perspective on disability or gender. There is someone writing a comic featuring a disabled superhero with a service dog. They run sensitivity questions by me. I read their work and help them with edits, with sensitive things so I can sit in that collaboration. [Note: Soul provided this kind of expert consultation to ensure the definitions in the glossary of *Being a Super Trans Ally!* (Schneider and Paris, 2020) would be accurate and current as of 2020.] My brother has been so helpful with my writing. He's an English major, so he sends me some articles. I send him what I've been working on, and he sends me some feedback. I provide him with feedback for his work. I really love my brother. He's so great! He's not afraid or shy to say, "I love you."

Reflection: Building support systems

What intrigues you about what Alise, Grayson, Helen and Soul shared about building support systems?

. . . .

. . . .

. . . .

Alise emphasizes "having people that you can really be yourself with. Even if it's just virtually..." Who can you smile and have fun with? Are there people you feel you can be fully yourself with? Does this happen for you virtually as well as in person?

. . . .

. . . .

. . . .

Where have you found connection, belonging and community? How do you build support systems? Do you already have people in your network or is this something you want to work on developing? Or is this not a priority for you?

. . . .

. . . .

. . . .

Tree hugger!

Building a support system can include natural elements. Go outside and find a new tree or visit a beloved tree. Acknowledge its magnificence. Thank the tree for the oxygen it produces as you breathe in deeply. Experience the tree's textures, colors, size, scent and energy. Use all of your senses. And, YES, put your arms around that tree in a hug! Love that tree! Alternatively, stand with your back against the tree and feel your spine uplifted or touch the tree with your hand or just feel the tree's presence without physical touch. You could also imagine or feel yourself growing roots like a tree. If there are no trees in your vicinity, find some wood where you are (floor, furniture, most paper, etc.) and send gratitude to the tree it once was, or find a picture of a tree that appeals to you.

And if anyone calls you a "tree hugger," you can proudly proclaim, "Yes, I am!" Maybe even add, "You should try it sometime."

Now, let's think more about human support.

Ally action!

We are about to learn the perspectives of Alise, Grayson, Helen and Soul on **how allies can help make a difference.**

Alise

I'm constantly asking myself how allies can help. One big action is just being there for your friends or being there for the person who's talking. I really appreciate people being gracious and saying, "Thank you for sharing." I've had experiences where people just want to delve in and analyze right away, but I really do appreciate it when people take that moment and say, "Thank you. I know that this is labor that you're doing and I really appreciate it." I always encourage allies to think about how much space they're taking up in discussions and in certain spaces. I think one thing that you should take away is knowing when to take up space and when to not— knowing what's appropriate, what's not; knowing if you're taking space from someone else, taking opportunity from someone else, being self-aware.

Grayson

So, broadly, allies, educate yourselves. Don't expect trans people to educate you. In an age where you have access to unlimited resources with the internet, and unlimited connections with people on the internet, there should be no reason why you should approach a trans person and ask them personal questions that they might not even know how to answer or feel uncomfortable answering. You could read literature, watch documentaries, listen to trans voices on any given platform. Stand by the trans people in your life. Boost their voices. Listen to them. Give them a space, a platform to share their voice. Sharing and asking for current name and pronouns is a huge thing. It's something that you can insert into your vocabulary very easily. It can be so scary correcting people on your pronouns or your identity as a trans person. Everyone sharing their pronouns acknowledges that

"I know why this is important and I know why I should be doing this." This is also giving a platform for trans and gender nonconforming people to share their pronouns, as otherwise they might be misgendered. If you see transphobia or people negatively enforcing the gender binary, call it in. Use your privilege as someone who's not trans to call it in.

When my school district's policy for inclusion and acceptance of trans and gender diverse students came out, right before I went into my junior year, I remember I was so happy to hear about it. For me, as someone who did not have that policy when I first came out but needed it, it was kind of a relief to me. We absolutely need those protections to be made by every single school district. Allies can work towards that.

Helen

I think the best allies ask the people they're being allies to what they need from them. And so, if that's amplifying someone's voice, if that's "I don't have the capacity to deal with this, can you deal with it?" or "Hey, can you talk to your community that you're from and do this because I just can't do that right now," that's all important. Quote someone, cite your sources. Read what people from marginalized communities have to say about things.  Encourage people to do more research. Don't get all your information about racial justice from white people.

It's painful and difficult to go through the process of learning about your privileges. And there is, for many people, a feeling that "Oh, well, if I have privilege that means my life hasn't been hard, but my life has been hard. Therefore, privilege is fake." And it takes some learning and education and listening. That's key: listening to what other people are saying and realizing how privilege operates. Because privilege is real, it doesn't mean that you haven't personally experienced suffering. It's just that certain identities you have may have protected you from kinds of suffering that other people are facing. Anyone who has privilege has to eventually have the experience of having their privilege checked. And having to realize that is sometimes really painful and you want to fight it and say, "No, but I'm a good person. I'm not bad." But you have to step back and think, "Well, just because I did this thing that was hurtful, that doesn't mean this person is saying I'm a bad person. They're just asking me to not do that thing again or to think critically about why I did it." And your sore, sad feelings of "but I'm good," you can take and talk to someone later about. Don't force a person who's marginalized to deal with your sad, hurt feelings. That's not okay. That's not their job. Sometimes we do things and they're hurtful even though we don't mean them to be. We may talk over people by accident, or use a word without knowing that it has a particular background, or we are really excited about a topic so we want to share a lot. And then we are told afterwards that we were taking up space in a way that we shouldn't have been. The best thing that we can do is to apologize and do better in the future.

Soul

Allies can help make a difference through direct action supporting people on artist funding sites, especially disabled artists, people who are doing their best to do the work. Vote, volunteer at food pantries, donate to service dog organizations—that is one that's very near and dear to my heart. I do think it's important to give people funding for that leg up as well. It is quite terrifying to be looking at how much a studio costs and what a huge dent that would make in the money I might have in savings—and I'm very lucky to have savings. Be a good person. Do that, too. Don't park your bike on the accessibility ramp. I can't speak for other non-binary people, but I do feel that this experience isn't solely mine. So, one thing that I'd say to people who are close to other non-binary people is use the primary pronouns they prefer over they/their/them. Go the extra mile. And, you know, it's really a way of stating, "You're cared about. I see you," beyond just using they/their/them because it's easier and more universal.

Reflection: Allyship

What are your take-aways from what Alise, Grayson, Helen and Soul shared about allyship? Are there ally actions you already practice that they mentioned? Are there some new strategies you plan to use?

. . . .

. . . .

. . . .

Grayson says pronouns are "a huge thing. It's something that you can insert into your vocabulary very easily." Soul encourages us to "Go the extra mile" and use all non-binary pronouns.

Let's delve into pronoun practice and some ideas about the gender binary.

Beyond the gender binary

Why do we assume things about people based on their clothing, voice, demeanor and hair? Who benefits from these conscious or unconscious expectations and assumptions? Consider the idea of only two genders. This is called the gender binary. It is constructed and enforced socially, which harms many people. Let's go beyond the gender binary. If you believe that there are only two genders and are invested in this belief, this may be challenging for you. Breathe through it. There are an infinite variety of ways that a person can identify and express their gender.

Gender **identity** means how we think about ourselves and how we feel. Gender **expression** is how we present ourselves to the world through our clothing, voice, hair, style and how we carry ourselves. Gender identity and gender expression are different things and it is often assumed that they are related and unchanging. How a person thinks about their gender (identity) may not be reflected in their style and demeanor (expression) especially since rigid gender norms are socially enforced and people may not feel safe to express themselves. Similarly, gender and sexual orientation are also two different things and we cannot assume they are related or unchanging.

We are working to create a world in which all people, including LGBTQ+ people, get to live fully in their truth. Unfortunately, there are attitudinal barriers (people's lack of acceptance and education about the issues), physical and emotional harms, and structural barriers (such as not having access to restrooms and locker rooms which align with one's gender identity).[1] LGBTQ+ people and especially gender diverse people have very real concerns about being shunned or harmed by family, friends and community members. We urgently need to change the ways that transgender and non-binary people are mistreated and denied opportunities in employment, housing, medical care and education.[2]

Fortunately, there is a growing awareness and acceptance of gender diversity and inclusivity. And there is beauty and joy in living in alignment with one's internal sense of self. One of the best ways we can show respect for a person is to address them by their current name and pronouns. Most people do not pause before assuming pronouns such as she/her/hers and he/him/his. When these "automatic" responses are incorrect (called misgendering), transgender, non-binary and gender expansive people can be harmed. It's important to be proficient with the pronoun "they" as a singular pronoun (even if, and especially if, you think it sounds unfamiliar or plural). You can get good at it (if you are not already). Let's practice!

"They" is here to stay!

Let's say you have a friend named V who identifies as genderqueer and uses "they" pronouns (they/their/them). What does V look like? What is V wearing? You can practice with V's pronouns by saying this story out loud as if you were telling the story to another friend. It may be tempting just to read this passage silently. Take the time to read it aloud. Pause as needed. Breathe life into the story. Read it out aloud multiple times if you need to, and continue getting comfortable with "they" as a singular pronoun.

V went to the market yesterday. They needed a few items to make their partner a fantastic dinner. V got to the register and realized they forgot their wallet at home. V was upset. They searched everywhere without finding it. The cashier said that they would have to leave their groceries and come back another time. V was frustrated but didn't think there was another option but to leave and come back. They were putting their groceries back into the cart to wheel to customer service when they heard someone call out to them. It was Alex! V's friend Alex happened to be in line a few people behind V. Alex offered her credit card to V. V was surprised and thanked her profusely and said they would pay her back. Alex said that wouldn't be necessary, that it was her gift towards their dinner because it was V's birthday month. V was so moved by that expression of generosity and love that they did a happy dance!

Debriefing: How did working with the pronoun "they" go for you?

. . . .

. . . .

. . . .

Did you wonder if V had a handbag/purse? Were you looking for signs to reveal if they were "really a woman" or "really a man"?[3] All gender identities are real and valid and do not require our "approval" to exist. Accept people for who they are, not based on the stories you may have imagined about them or the limiting stories the gender binary has constructed for all of us.

Fun with fae/faer/fen!

Let's practice using both they/their/them and fae/faer/fen pronouns!

Complete this activity two times. It is a true story about our friend Soul who is featured throughout the book. This first time, fill in the blanks using they/their/them pronouns (options: they/them/their/theirs/themselves, each of which is used at least once). Say the completed sentences out loud.

Soul's glass bouquets

Soul (pronouns they/their/them) made a video called "Creating Self Portrait (2019) an Installation of Glass Flowers"[4] to document the creation of . . . . Bachelor of Fine Arts (BFA) project at the glass workshop. Let's go and watch the video to journey with . . . . ! It's fascinating to see how Soul shows . . . . in action as . . . . go through the elaborate process of lost wax casting to create a hundred glass flower bouquets! Once we see Soul's gorgeous glass work, we immediately recognize the piece as . . . . because the bouquets are arranged in the shape of . . . . scars, which is a stylemark of Soul's art. What do . . . . call the video? "My Scars are Art."

Next, fill in the blanks using fae/faer/fen pronouns (options: fae/fen/faer/faers/faerself, each of which is used at least once). Say the completed sentences out loud.

Soul (pronouns fae/faer/fen) made a video called "Creating Self Portrait (2019) an Installation of Glass Flowers" to document the creation of . . . . BFA project at the glass workshop. Let's go and watch the video to journey with . . . . ! It's fascinating to see how Soul shows . . . . in action as . . . . goes through the elaborate process of lost wax casting to create a hundred glass flower bouquets! Once we see Soul's gorgeous glass work, we immediately recognize the piece as . . . . because the bouquets are arranged in the shape of . . . . scars, which is a stylemark of Soul's art. What does . . . . call the video? "My Scars are Art."

There are many other pronouns! Try this activity again and again using no pronouns (name only), ze/hir pronouns, or the pronouns your non-binary friend, family member, co-worker or community member uses.

For more ways to take action towards creating a world that works for people of all genders, explore and engage with the activities in *Being a Super Trans Ally! A Creative Workbook and Journal for Young People*[5] (and older people, too!).

Answer key for both they/their/them and fae/faer/fen pronouns for comparison

Soul made a video called "Creating Self Portrait (2019) an Installation of Glass Flowers" to document the creation of **their/faer** BFA project at the glass workshop. Let's go and watch the video to journey with **them/fen**! It's fascinating to see how Soul shows **themself/fenself*** in action as **they/fae** go(es) through the elaborate process of lost wax casting to create 100 glass flower bouquets! Once we see Soul's gorgeous glass work, we immediately recognize the piece as **theirs/faers** because the bouquets are arranged in the shape of **their/faer** scars, which is a stylemark of Soul's art. What do(es) **they/fae** call the video? "My Scars are Art."

*Note: some people use "faerself" instead of "fenself."

CHAPTER 6
SELF-CARE

How is your self-care practice?

- ❏ What self-care practice?!? I don't know what self-care is. It sounds self-indulgent or selfish or something

- ❏ I don't have time to take care of myself. I'm busy helping others

- ❏ I have a little self-care time a few times a year

- ❏ I tried self-care but it wasn't for me

- ❏ I prioritize and practice self-care daily

- ❏ Write in: ....

Every day is a great day to take care of yourself! It is not selfish or only for certain kinds of people. It is about recognizing your needs and taking care of your body, mind and spirit. Productivity pressures and systems of oppression often take us out of ourselves. Can we make friends with ourselves, slow down and listen in to see what is best for us? We can do that in every moment. Self-care is not about buying products or services (but sometimes those can be helpful). It's about connecting deeply with ourselves and others who are making a difference in the world and in their own lives.

Are you curious about how Alise, Grayson, Helen and Soul practice **self-care**? Let's hear directly from them!

Alise

I practice self-care with mindfulness, music and writing. I started going to a mindfulness club in my junior year. Being able to take a step back and read and take time for myself and just notice how I was feeling really uplifted my mental health. It helped me take care of myself and notice when I was getting super drained and realize what things made me feel that way. So, to this day when I can't focus, I try to take time and use a mindfulness app. Later, I co-led the mindfulness club at school. So, every Tuesday morning, even if I kind of fell off the wagon with mindfulness, I'd take that 30 minutes of just being with other people and then a ten-minute practice, centering myself and reminding myself this is something I like to do and can make time for, even if I don't feel I have time for it. "The shame and stigma shut down" process reminds me of loving-kindness meditation practices, which have helped me so much and are so beautiful!

Listening to music that I like helps me either feel my emotions or just soothe me. I really like listening to music when I feel overwhelmed or just frustrated. Especially at school, there were times when I just felt so tense. During lunch, I would go to a music practice room and practice my saxophone and it was really nice. It helped me realize that there are things I do other than studying and being stressed. Sax quartet is honestly a really big highlight of high school. Music takes my mind off of everything else because I have to focus on it so much.

Writing, normally, is an act of self-care for me. It was really hard for me to do until I was stuck inside my house during the pandemic, because it takes so much. For me, writing is super heavy and processing and there was a lot I didn't really want to process.

Grayson

I do a ton of self-care actually. I struggle a lot with my mental health, all the time. I suffer a lot with my anxiety disorder as well as some other illnesses. And so I have to spend a lot of time taking care of myself. The number-one thing that I have had to learn with self-care is that it's okay to take care of yourself. That's where you have to start because humans in general feel guilty for being selfish; but there's nothing selfish about taking care

of yourself. It's the number-one priority. I've always loved the analogy that you need to put on your own oxygen mask before someone else's. The main way that I take care of myself is just making time to get all the things that are in my head out. I have a lot of thoughts, just about life in general, but also about activism. I have filled up journal upon journal with just my thoughts, because when they're all stuck up here in my head, it gets cloudy. It gets scary. It gets overwhelming. And even if that outlet is sharing it with other people, that's still creating change. So, the main way I take care of myself is just getting my thoughts out into the world, which in turn might help other people.

Helen

I read a lot. I try to do my nails because it is a calming thing that I like and keeps me feeling that I have a ritual in my life. I try to be in touch with the world around me. Every time I see the full moon, I light a candle for her. I follow the Wheel of the Year, which is a pagan set of holidays, and I celebrate those. I try to be thankful and think about the things that I'm lucky to have in my life. I have a really strong support network of friends who

encourage me to take care of myself and reach out to me about eating okay and getting out of the house, and I also see a therapist once a week. I try really hard to have good sleep hygiene. I've been fostering kittens, and that's been really wonderful. Watching kittens grow and learn and develop is really beautiful, and they're super cute.

Soul

Mental health treatment plans are more than just therapy and drugs. Part of my specific treatment plan is meditation. I have a meditation that I try to do at night. It's just a time to unwind. I diffuse the scent of lavender in my room before going to bed because sleep hygiene is something that I really struggle with and not getting enough sleep has been very damaging to my health. And I drink a lot of tea. I have a special morning tea. I have afternoon tea, and I have "it's time to go to sleep" tea. Yoga and physical therapy really help me on a physical level. I walk and cuddle my retired service dog Branka. That's why she's an emotional support animal because she's an important part of a mental health treatment plan. Being in nature is really helpful. I want to build a garden. I go out every once in a while with my camera and I take pictures of all the flowers that are blooming, of the birds, trying to find the rabbits.

Positive self-talk has been really important too, because sometimes my brain just thinks something negative and something hurtful about me, without my permission. I say out loud, "No, I don't deserve this negative thought. I am good." And I sit down in the evening, and in the morning, and plan, which has been a really helpful part of my ten-minutes thing. I sit down and I say, "Why is working on my website important to me? What do I need to do tomorrow?" I make my whole little list of everything every morning and remind myself, "Why is it important and what am I going to do?" This kind of wakes me up and reminds me what the meaning of my life is. And I share my enthusiasm with my parents, through editing these videos, even though it's really hard. And I look at my accomplishments and even my setbacks with love and caring. With my depression, I've always had an extremely hard time feeling accomplished. Now, when I finish something and I don't feel accomplished, instead of being frustrated or beating myself up about it, I just say to myself, "Oh, I'm not going to feel this way." The book *Radical Acceptance*[1] talks about turning to those emotions and saying, "Welcome. Yes. You." To look at them with love and caring. That's really helped me so much lately.

Reflection: Self-care

Grayson reminds us that, "There's nothing selfish about taking care of yourself. It's the number-one priority." Alise shares, "Centering myself and reminding myself this is something I like to do and can make time for, even if I don't feel I have time for it." What are your thoughts about what was shared about self-care?

. . . .

. . . .

. . . .

Alise mentions mindfulness. In *My Anxiety Handbook*, Knowles, Gallagher and McEwen say, "Mindfulness is a technique that can help us to calm our thoughts and focus on the present moment."[2] If you are looking for mindfulness practices, there are so many out there (including some in this book). Explore lots of options and discover what works best for you.

Here are the self-care practices Alise, Grayson, Helen and Soul described. Put a check mark (✓) next to practices you already use. Put a star/asterisk (*) next to anything you are inspired to try.

Alise's self-care practices

❏ Getting centered

❏ Listening to music

❏ Noticing how I'm feeling

❏ Noticing what things make me feel drained (or energized)

❏ Playing music

❏ Practicing mindfulness

❏ Using a mindfulness app

❏ Reading

❏ Taking a step back

❏ Taking time for myself

❏ Writing

Grayson's self-care practices

- ❏ Journal writing
- ❏ Sharing thoughts with others
- ❏ Taking time to record thoughts

Helen's self-care practices

- ❏ Being there for friends
- ❏ Connecting with support people
- ❏ Connecting with the natural world
- ❏ Cultivating communication with friends
- ❏ Doing things that foster happiness
- ❏ Eating well
- ❏ Enjoying kittens
- ❏ Getting out of the house
- ❏ Practicing feeling grateful
- ❏ Lighting a candle for the moon (ceremonial practices)
- ❏ Manicuring nails
- ❏ Not self-isolating
- ❏ Reading (same with Alise)
- ❏ Seeing a therapist
- ❏ Sleeping well
- ❏ Verbalizing feelings

Soul's self-care practices

- ❏ Being in nature
- ❏ Diffusing the scent of lavender
- ❏ Dog walking and cuddling
- ❏ Doing yoga
- ❏ Drinking tea
- ❏ Focusing on what is important and why
- ❏ Growing a garden
- ❏ Looking at accomplishments and setbacks with love and caring
- ❏ Meditating (Alise's practice, too!)
- ❏ Physical therapy
- ❏ Planning and making lists

❏ Practicing positive self-talk and compassionately challenging negative self-talk

❏ Reminding oneself about the meaning of life

❏ Sharing enthusiasm with others

❏ Taking pictures

Sherry's self-care practices

Adding to what was already shared:

❏ Dancing

❏ Drawing

❏ Holding crystals

❏ Laughing

❏ Learning

❏ Listening

❏ Loving

❏ Practicing body awareness

❏ Resting/napping

❏ Taking walks

What self-care practices are you using that are not already included on the lists? Maybe baking, cooking, crafting, gardening, taking baths, playing games or physical fitness (lifting weights, etc.)?

. . . .

. . . .

What self-care practices did you mark as ones you would like to try? How will you incorporate these into your schedule? Give yourself a month to make a new practice a habit. If you try a new practice and it does not feel helpful, give yourself permission to let it go. If the new practice feels good, try it for an additional month.

Self-care activities

Who's in your corner? You are!

How often through the day are you pausing to be mindful of what is happening in your body and breath? Are there ways that you can partner with yourself? Are you practicing witnessing yourself, having compassion for yourself and taking time for yourself? Let's give it a try!

Here are some statements you can say aloud or write in a journal. How you feel in the moment is important and how you feel later may be different.

Witnessing myself: "I witness what is happening to you, ... (your name). I stand with myself. I believe in myself. I am important to me."

Witnessing another person (or yourself in the third person or a group of people): "I witness what is happening to you, ... (person's name). I stand with you. I believe in you. You are important to me."

How did that go for you?

. . . .

. . . .

. . . .

If it's your first time with this kind of witnessing, it may feel unfamiliar. Keep at it!

If you are experiencing an issue related to injustice, recognize how it is affecting (showing up in) your body. Acknowledge the immediate situation, your body's response and how it is connected to a bigger picture of social systems at play.

Trust your body. Honor its wisdom. Try asking these questions about your body's response: Where do you feel it in your body? How strong is the feeling? Is there a color, texture or sensation associated with the situation?

Next, bring your awareness to the room or place (setting) where your body is located. What colors do you see around you? What textures? If possible, look at your pinky finger. Wiggle it around if you are able. If not, please imagine this exercise happening. See if that little finger will move around in the air so it looks like it is tracing an imaginary circle. Try it with the other pinky finger if possible. Try it with both pinky fingers at the same time. Relax your pinky and try to get your index finger to trace a circle. Is that easier or more challenging? Just notice without judgment.

Where can the power be found within yourself? Is there positive resource in your body? A resiliency message?

. . . .

. . . .

. . . .

What if you are stressed or feeling exhausted? What helps? Check any of the strategies you use (✓):

- ❏ Knowing it's okay to say no

- ❏ Taking care of yourself

- ❏ Asking for help

- ❏ Having boundaries about what you are and are not willing to do

- ❏ Staying energized

- ❏ Getting rest

- ❏ Acknowledging what you are grateful for

- ❏ Leaning into the support of community

- ❏ Noticing achievements and what is going well (even if it might also be true that there is still so much more to do and things that are not going well)

- ❏ Remembering your power

❏   Honoring the memory and efforts of those who came before us

❏   What else? ....

Let's take some time to emphasize the positive!

Highlight your contributions

It's often easier to remember challenges than it is to hold on to triumphs. Why is that? As humans, we are wired to highlight and recall dangers so that we may avoid them. It's like looking at a page in a book where some text has been highlighted (the dangers). The non-highlighted text is still there but it's easy to overlook it in favor of what is highlighted.

Let's work on developing the skill of emphasizing the positive. It takes time, energy and perseverance to make this a habit that sticks. It's so easy to allow the default setting of highlighting the dangers and difficulties. Think of a time when you took an action that made a difference. Can you recall several such actions you took? Ideas include helping a person/people, animals, or the Earth, speaking/standing up for justice, listening/witnessing, being creative, donating time/money/resources, expressing your care and concern, and so much more.

This process is just for you. It does not need to be broadcast publicly (or it can be if you would like). It might be a good exercise to publicly acknowledge others for their contributions and describe how they make a difference. This is about noticing and appreciating yourself and building your capacity for sustainable action and self-care.

Actions I have taken that made a difference
Situation 1: Briefly describe the situation. What action did you take? How did your action make a difference?

....

....

....

How do you feel as you recall Situation 1? How is your breathing? How does your heart feel? What do your eyes see or ears hear?

. . . .

. . . .

. . . .

Embody ("anchor in") the good feeling of making a difference. If you are able and willing to do so, breathe in and out a few times while looking at your hands and thinking about how you made a difference.

Situation 2: Briefly describe the situation. What action did you take? How did your action make a difference?

. . . .

. . . .

. . . .

How do you feel as you recall Situation 2? What is your mind thinking? How do your hands feel?

. . . .

. . . .

. . . .

Again, embody the good feeling of making a difference. Breathe deeply.

Situation 3: Briefly describe the situation. What action did you take? How did your action make a difference?

....

....

....

How do you feel as you recall Situation 3? What temperature is your body experiencing right now? How do your feet feel? How hungry are you?

....

....

....

Embody the good feeling of making a difference again. If possible, gently sway from side to side as you breathe deeply.

Acknowledging myself

Let's use our "Actions I have taken that made a difference" situations to write a poem, story, song or rap! We'll consider a sample first and then play with the action scenarios you completed to generate your own creation in three steps.

Part 1: Write what is most essential from each action situation (this is a sample)

Situation 1: I helped my younger sibling with their homework.
My breathing is relaxed. My heart feels at peace.

Situation 2: I made masks for essential workers during the early days of the global pandemic.
My mind thinks I did a good job. My hands feel accomplished.

Situation 3: I learned new strategies for helping manage anxiety with mindfulness and movement. I posted a video of myself using those practices. My friend said it helped them.
My body feels tingly waves. My feet feel hot.

Part 2: Pick out key words from Part 1 above. Record the key words
Helped, sibling, homework, relaxed, peace, making masks, essential workers, accomplished, new strategies, anxiety, mindfulness, movement, friend, helped, tingly waves, feet, hot.

Part 3: Turn those words into a poem, story, song or rap!
Homework-helping sibling breathes easier
Mask-making hands keep workers safer
My hot feet move anxiety

Now, it's your turn!

Part 1: Write what is most essential from each of your "Actions I have taken that made a difference" situations
Situation 1 action and feeling(s):

. . . .

. . . .

Situation 2 action and feeling(s):

. . . .

. . . .

Situation 3 action and feeling(s):

. . . .

. . . .

Part 2: Pick out key words from Part 1. Record the key words

. . . .

. . . .

Part 3: Turn those words into a poem, story, song or rap!

. . . .

. . . .

. . . .

. . . .

Now it's time to celebrate your self-acknowledgments!

Part 4: Sing it out loud!

Dance it and feel alive with the joy of making a difference! Sing your song/ poem/story often and write new verses whenever you want to celebrate your accomplishments. Consider recording yourself singing your song and playing it back for yourself when needed.

Doesn't it feel good to make a difference and to do so in a way that honors yourself in the process? This helps remind us to keep love, joy and self-care in mind as we work towards justice in society.

CHAPTER 7
SUPPORT, ENCOURAGEMENT AND FUTURE INTENTIONS

Let's hear from Alise, Grayson, Helen and Soul about who **supports, encourages** and **collaborates** with each of them.

Alise

The biggest person in my life who supports me is my mom. She's my best friend. She's always there for me. I can tell her anything and she makes sure that I know that I can tell her anything, with no judgment. She's there for me, which is just really nice to have. I'm super grateful for my mom. She's just amazing. I love her so much. Whenever I feel upset or discouraged, she's always there to push me when I need it, but she's also there just to hold me when I need it. I really appreciate that.

In my freshman year of high school and then also my junior year through Young Playwrights, I found a really awesome community in Vashti Dubois, who is the keeper of the Colored Girls Museum,[1] and that's her house. In activism, I think I found most of my collaborators in Diversity Trainers because that's what the space is for. It was really nice to find people who knew how it was and how it was supposed to be and were determined to try to be there in those conversations. I do find support in clubs at school, just people who are socially motivated and people who are super aware of history and society and things that are going on today.

Grayson

Many people support me: the GSA, the student council, and the people who opened up a pathway for me to come in as a presenter. There are a lot of different ways that you can support someone. My mom has shown me more than anyone else how people can change. That is incredibly inspirational to me because when I first came out, she had no idea what transgender meant. She had never even heard the term before. She had to look it  up on the internet. [Laughs] Watching her grow has been so wonderful; seeing her start coming to Pride events with me and sit in the first row for all my presentations and become an advocate. She's on a group on social media for parents of trans kids. She has become such an advocate for me and for my community and we need more people like that. She's definitely someone who has supported me and stood behind me.

There are smaller ways that you can support people, as I mentioned earlier about the principal using his pronouns. That's not going up to you and saying, "I support you," but it's still showing support in the community. And it is a way of communicating that "I'm here for you. I'm a safe person." The allies are such an important part of the movement. There are many ways that people support you and collaborate with you on different projects you're trying to do or different initiatives inside your community. I've met so many people along my path who stood by me whether they were silent about it or told me about it.

Helen

Who supports me? Definitely you, Sherry, but also my friends, my partner. My parents are really quite supportive of the fact that I'm teaching. I think the content of what I'm teaching about gay erotica is less exciting to them, but they're supportive of the fact that I'm doing things that I find meaningful.

Soul

My parents and my siblings are my most important supporters. To a lesser extent, there are the friends that I'm only in contact with online. We go to the Glass Art Society (GAS) conference, which is a huge opportunity to network. I think I'm a pretty introverted person. I spend so much emotional energy there that my dad has to take me because of my disabilities, which raises the price a lot. We stay at the area for extra time, so I can recharge before going through the difficulty of going home. At GAS networking events where they give us food and stuff, I am jumping from person to person explaining my work, handing out printouts of my work, listening to their work, just having supportive and inspiring conversations.

Reflection: Who supports, encourages and collaborates with you?

Who supports, encourages and collaborates with you? How do they do that?

....

....

....

Who do you support, encourage and collaborate with? How do you do that?

....

....

....

Developing my support network

Do you already have people in your life who support and honor you? Fantastic! Are you working to develop more relationships that are accepting and affirming? Way to go! Seek out people who like and love and celebrate you for who you are and all that you are, and welcome people as they are in the fullness of their truth. Can you identify what you need to feel respected and supported? Let's get to it!

What do you need? Check as many as apply (✓).

- ❏ To be heard/seen/known
- ❏ To be affirmed for all I am
- ❏ To grow
- ❏ To write
- ❏ To create (art)
- ❏ To sing or create music
- ❏ To take a walk or be in nature
- ❏ To move/dance/exercise
- ❏ To cook/bake
- ❏ To read
- ❏ To learn

- ❏ To play (games)
- ❏ To laugh
- ❏ To practice mindfulness
- ❏ To rest
- ❏ To attend conferences/lectures
- ❏ To attend protests/rallies/demonstrations
- ❏ To love and be loved
- ❏ To be inspired (what inspires you?)
- ❏ To grieve or mourn

What else do you need? Write in: . . . .

Which of the things on the needs list would you like to do with another person or other people? Put a star/asterisk (*) next to those items.

Now write your ideal "support person/network request advertisement."

I am seeking a support person/friend/partner/date/ally to:

. . . .

. . . .

. . . .

Let's figure out what to do with this advertisement:

1. Say it out loud to set your intention
2. Post it in the school or community newspaper. Perhaps the editors of the paper could invite anyone who wants to create these request ads
3. Post it on social media

Friends with yourself?

Did you include yourself in your support network? Yes? Fantastic! If it didn't occur to you, don't worry. It's not a common practice or even an idea most people would have. We have a great resource within us: our heart and body! Learning to pay attention to our heart and body can be a source of energy and a free and easily accessible resource available to us at any time. Could you invite yourself to be your friend? Could you treat yourself as you would treat a friend, such as offering kind and encouraging words, support, positive intentions (wanting the best for your friend/self), and seeing the good about your friend (yourself)? Ask yourself, "Am I treating myself as I would treat a friend?" So often, we are much harder on ourselves than we would be on our friends. Can we offer ourselves the same compassion and care we offer others?

Ask your body!

Your body is a great resource! Body wisdom is here to help you. Pause, breathe and lean into the energy of your body now. Listen in!

Foot notes

Note: If you cannot or prefer not to work with your feet or do not have feet, please work with a different body part and insert the name of that part in the blank space.

What supports do we have as we move through the world? Many people can say "my feet"! Many people can say "my mobility device" (cane, walker, wheelchair, crutches or scooter)! How often do you pay attention to your feet/.................. or your mobility device? How are your feet/.................. feeling right now? Give gratitude to your feet/.................. for all they do and acceptance for what they don't do. If possible, touch or massage your feet/.................. Use your imagination to send your breath to your feet/.................. Be with your feet/.................. If possible, look at them with love and compassion. Ask your feet/.................. what they need and want. Record any wisdom your feet/.................. have to share or write your feet/.................. or mobility device a love note.

....

....

....

If you have use of your feet/.................. this way, write a love note on the floor with your big toe/.................. (in invisible ink!). Sit on a chair if you would like to try this exercise with both toes/.................. at the same time. You could also imagine writing on the ceiling (more invisible ink!) with your toes/.................. if you lie on your back on the floor or bed. If you are using both feet/.................. at the same time, does the writing look like mirror images? Experiment! Have fun!

Let's think more about support and consider what is helpful and unhelpful.

Holding space for a person

Have you ever had someone "be there for you" in a way that really helped? Or in a way you hoped would help but that was somehow less than supportive or really hurt? Briefly describe that experience or those experiences:

. . . .

. . . .

. . . .

How we respond to a person who is sharing their experience can make a huge difference. Are you adding to a person's difficulty or helping them move through it?

   If your friend or loved one is upset about an experience of (check any or all) (✓):

❏ Racism/racialization

❏ Sexism

❏ Classism

❏ Homophobia/biphobia/
   queerphobia

❏ Transphobia

❏ Ableism

❏ Saneism

❏ Ageism

❏ Sizeism

❏ Xenophobia (religious bias,
   anti-immigration bias, any
   bias based on difference)

❏ Write in: . . . .

How do you proceed? Does a particular situation come to mind? Briefly describe a time when someone shared something important with you:

. . . .

. . . .

. . . .

Does this sound supportive?

Classify each of the responses in the chart as Supportive (+), Neutral (=) or Unsupportive (–) by putting a check mark (✓) or the sign (+, =, –) in the corresponding box.

+	=	-	Statement
			1. "I can understand why you are upset."
			2. "You're being too sensitive."
			3. "It's no big deal. It couldn't have been that bad."
			4. "Okay."
			5. "Thank you for sharing your experience/perspective (with me)."
			6. "Stop complaining. It could be a lot worse."
			7. "I hear you."
			8. "I/they didn't mean it. That was not my/their intention."
			9. "I see."
			10. "I believe you."
			11. "I am listening."
			12. "That's concerning."
			13. "That's not what happened. There is no problem."
			14. "You did not deserve that."
			15. "I'm here for you."

Practice saying the supportive statements and the neutral statements out loud. Use your "Shame and stigma shut down" technique to flag the statements that are unsupportive when you hear them being said to you or others. Let's keep considering how to be supportive.

Answer key for "Does this sound supportive?"
Supportive statements (+): 1, 10, 12, 14, 15 (and maybe 5, 7, 11)

Unsupportive statements (–): 2, 3, 6, 8, 13

Neutral statements (=): 4, 5, 7, 9, 11

Three supportive steps

What would you do if a friend, family member or even an acquaintance shared with you their experience of an incident? Here are three supportive steps for you to consider: 1. Listen and validate; 2. Offer support; and 3. Take action on your support offer.

1. **Listen and validate the person's/people's feelings and concerns.** Hold space for the person/people to express themselves (if that is what they want) while you listen unconditionally. Respect their process and dignity. Keep confidentiality (unless help is needed because the person is being harmed or is considering harming themselves or others, in which case please discuss your concerns with the person and collaborate on a plan to get support).

2. **Offer support.** That could include saying: "I'm here for you." "How can I best support you?" "I want to support you. Here are some options. Which would be most useful to you right now?" "Please call on me to..." (Check the options you are willing and able to offer ✓.)

❏   Listen and hold space for you

❏   Brainstorm/strategize about how you want to proceed

❏   Help educate others/spread the word

❏   Talk to the person/people who said or did something offensive/ harmful (if it is safe/appropriate to do so)

❏   Go with you to report the incident

❏   Work to create change at the personal level

❏   Work to create change at the policy level

❏   Be here for you through the process as it unfolds

❏   Help you connect to other support

❏   Check in with you again later or another time

❏   What else? . . . .

3. **Take action:** [Note: Be sure to secure consent from the person who experienced the incident before sharing their name/story.] (Check the actions you are willing and able to do ✓.)

❏   Follow through on offers of support

❏   Collaborate with other allies to take action

❏   Stand with/up, speak up/out

❏   Keep on educating yourself

❏   Hold individuals and groups accountable by calling them in/out

❏   Write letters or make phone calls as needed

❏   Sign/start a petition

❏   Create a survey to determine what others have experienced and share the results

❏   Organize an event/conference/protest/demonstration/rally

❏   Collect funds for organizers or to donate to the cause

❏   What other action(s) might be needed?

. . . .

. . . .

. . . .

We'll consider more actions in Chapter 9.

What did they say? That's not okay! The opposite of support

Just as it's useful to recognize what support looks like and sounds like, it's also useful to be familiar with the opposite of support. Here are some examples (italicized items are from the previous chart activity called "Does this sound supportive?") Check any of the items that you have experienced before (✓) (on the giving or receiving end):

- ❏ Denying (*"That's not what happened. There is no problem."*)

- ❏ Minimizing (*"It's no big deal. It couldn't have been that bad."*)

- ❏ Shaming/blaming/judgment ("I can't believe you did that! What's wrong with you?")

- ❏ Mocking/laughing at the upset person ("Ha ha! She told you!")

- ❏ Demanding a response ("Get over it.")

- ❏ Pressuring the person to share vulnerable details ("Why won't you tell me?")

- ❏ Gossiping about what was shared and entrusted to your care ("Can you believe it? I just heard...")

- ❏ Defending the other party/situation/system ("You don't know what the other person is going through. They are nice people, so they can't be prejudiced. Everyone has equal opportunities.")

- ❏ Shifting focus ("Oh, that's nothing! Listen to what happened to me.")

- ❏ Changing the topic without acknowledgment ("Oh, speaking of . . . . , I bought a new shirt.")

- ❏ Giving unsolicited advice ("You should..." "You shouldn't..." "You need to...")

❏   Delaying or denying urgency ("Wait. We can't bring that forward now. There are other more pressing issues.")

❏   Dividing and conquering (Pitting people against each other, creating rivalries so people do not join forces and challenge those in power.)

❏   DARVO (Deny, Attack, and Reverse Victim and Offender) As Psychology Professor Jennifer J. Freyd, Ph.D., describes, "when an actually guilty perpetrator assumes the role of 'falsely accused' and attacks the accuser's credibility and blames the accuser of being the perpetrator of a false accusation."[2]

For the items you checked as having experienced, what response would you have wanted to receive (or give) in the situation? What would you have done differently (if anything)? How might you proceed in the future if you experience the opposite of support?

. . . .

. . . .

. . . .

Those uncomfortable conversations with friends and family members

Requesting a language correction (or perspective shift or behavior change) from someone in your life can feel like a big obstacle that is best avoided. With practice, it gets more familiar (and maybe even easier). So, let's run a role play! Perhaps the friend or family member has not considered their language or actions before. Perhaps they have been listening to others who have biased perspectives. Perhaps they have deep convictions based on prejudice. Could hearing from you make a difference? Let's hope so! Consider a conversation with your friend/family member (FFM) a fact-finding mission. What are their perspectives and

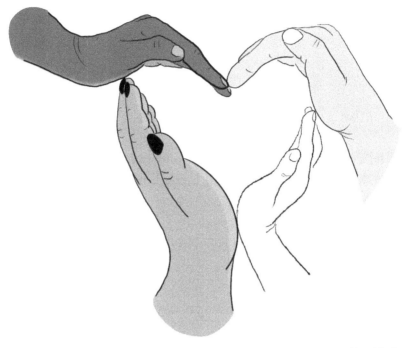

Heart in hands

prejudices? Are they open to considering other perspectives? Does it matter to them that you are concerned about social justice because you see how harmful injustice is? It is worth exploring and speaking up, even if it does not result in changed behavior. Your voice matters!

All scenes are generic so you can insert your own specifics about language or behavior.

Let's start with a person who is open to your request:

You: Hey, I appreciate that you are thoughtful about what you say and how you say it. I heard you say . . . . the other day. When I hear that language, I feel . . . . (upset, confused, etc.). So, I'd like to request that you . . . . (use a different word/expression or reframe the comment, etc.) in the future.

FFM: Oh, wow. Thank you for bringing that to my attention. I can definitely change the way I explain that in the future.

You: Thank you. I really appreciate your open response and willingness to make a change.

End scene. *Note:* If you have a suggestion for language that is more respectful, consider sharing that! ("I'd love to share with you some language that is considered more respectful. It's ....")

Next, let's consider talking to a person who may challenge your request. Notice the use of validation, humor and side-stepping of what could be perceived as insults.

You: Hey, could I share something with you?

FFM: What's up?

You: There's some language I'd like to talk about. What I heard you say earlier was offensive.

FFM: That's just how I talk. I don't mean it in an offensive way.

You: I can understand that you don't intend it in an offensive way but the impact is hurtful. What does that language mean to you? What do you think it means to other people?

FFM: It doesn't mean anything. You're overreacting. Stop being so sensitive.

You: This is important. I'm not comfortable with that language and what it represents.

FFM: I have a right to free speech, you know.

You: Of course you do. That's an important right which we both hold dear.

FFM: So, what's your point?

You: While we are at liberty to say what we want, we might consider using other language. Let's respect people who are harmed by the ways words and concepts perpetuate negative stereotypes and play into painful histories.

FFM: But those people aren't here right now, so why do I have to censor myself?

You: Perhaps instead of considering it censorship, consider it respect or courtesy. I respect you and think that you respect me, too. I value our relationship.

FFM: Yes, but what does that have to do with what I say?

You: When I hear that language, I think of people (I care about) being harmed. That upsets me.

FFM: Why do you care?

You: I'm helping create a world that works for all people.

FFM: You're a dreamer.

You: Yes, and I'd appreciate if you could help me in this small way towards realizing my dream. [Laughs]

FFM: I can't guarantee I won't use that language but I'll keep your campaign in mind.

You: Thank you. That means a lot to me. And I will keep reminding you about my dream.

End scene.

Finally, let's work with someone who is unwilling to consider your request.

You: Hey, I heard you say . . . . the other day. When I hear that language, I feel . . . . (upset, confused, etc.). So, I'd like to request that you . . . . (use a different word/expression or reframe the comment, etc.) in the future.

FFM: That's ridiculous. I'm not going to be controlled by your demands. Don't tell me how to talk.

You: I would appreciate your consideration for my request. Perhaps we can circle back around it another time.

FFM: I'm entitled to my perspective. You don't get to choose what I say or do. Don't try to change me. Let's just agree to disagree. [Walks away.]

End scene. Ouch. Please connect with support.

Role-play reflection

How did each of those scenes go for you?

....

....

....

Is there another perspective you'd like to play out? Write your own scene!

....

....

....

Great job practicing responding. Take time to pause, breathe and feel. In the next chapter, we'll continue reflecting and practicing as we consider apologies.

REACT-ing

How do we **REACT** when someone invites us to check our privilege or calls us in/out? It's great to respond from a compassionate place rather than having an automatic or hasty defensive reaction. This acrostic may help:

R = Reflect

E = Educate yourself*

A = Acknowledge the impact

C = Commit to doing better

T = Talk to people who support you and help keep you accountable**

* Don't expect people with marginalized identities to do further emotional labor to educate you.

** People who help keep you accountable are those who you trust to tell you the truth about how your privilege may obscure your understanding of the situation.

Do you admire how certain people respond or take proactive action?

My role models

Who are your current and historical role models? List them below. You can name individuals or groups of people. Your role models do not need to be famous. They are probably people who have made a difference to you personally (in your life, your thinking, your communities) or on a local, national or international scale. (Some people have no role models. Some people have lots of role models. If you need more space, please use your journal.)

. . . .

. . . .

. . . .

What **actions** do/did they take to make a difference?

....

....

....

In what ways do they **inspire** you?

....

....

....

Now, **tell them how they make a difference to you!** Share what you wrote about how their actions inspire you or express your gratitude in a creative way. If the person or people are not in your immediate circle or if they are not currently living, consider writing a tribute to them. Share it with friends, family and on social media if desired.

Learn from history and current movements

To learn about historical events and people, start by using the internet to search for a particular social movement or social justice issue and see if leaders or activists are named. For example, what is the inception of the annual LGBTQ+ Pride parades? Look up the Stonewall Riots, and the names Marsha P. Johnson and Sylvia Rivera. What sparked the creation of Black Lives Matter by co-founders Alicia Garza, Opal Tometi and Patrisse Cullors? Who are some current and historical Indigenous leaders? What actions are Latinx leaders taking towards justice for workers? How are LGBTQ+ Asian/Pacific Islander leaders challenging racism, bias and discrimination? Who is involved in the Disability Justice Movement? Who is working toward ending the Prison Industrial Complex? When you find the names of intriguing leaders, movements and communities, read all you can. See if there are videos to watch or books to read about the current or historical movement, especially by the leaders. Whenever possible, reference sources created by people with lived experience. Check out the *400 Years of Inequality Timeline*[3] which represents the history of African Americans, Indigenous peoples, women and working people in the United States visually and in text.

Remember those who have devoted their lives to making a difference and know that you are in good company. Know that your actions towards social justice make your role models proud! Carry their energy with you into your current and future pursuits.

And speaking of the future, are you curious about what intentions Alise, Grayson, Helen and Soul have for the **future** (as of June 2021)? Read on!

Alise

I'm in college with a double major in American Studies and film. I've thought about doing law work for non-profits. That's something that I've been really interested in. I've also thought about doing documentary work for news outlets. I think that's really cool. But any way that I can tie in my passion for writing and my passion for social justice is what I'm going for— and advocating for people and not getting caught up in politics, which could be super bureaucratic and not gratifying. I'm just trying to find ways that I can help people.

Grayson

I am currently a college student studying psychology, leadership and ethical development, and pre-medical studies. When I got my top surgery, I actually decided that I want to be a doctor. The first time I saw my chest after that surgery, I knew that feeling was what I wanted to give to others for the rest of my life. My ultimate goal is to end up a plastic surgeon or something similar to that. But, nonetheless, I'll be creating change in some way.

Helen

I'm planning to become a sex therapist. That's my end goal, hopefully. I'm definitely interested in working with individuals, couples and groups. I'd be interested in doing larger education workshops for people, perhaps writing curricula. I'm so excited to educate people. I plan to go immediately from undergrad to grad school. I'm trying to get a graduate degree in sexuality studies and then do private practice after that. That would be the dream.

Soul

I am creating the in-home studio that I need to be able to continue my work in a way that's accessible and best for my health. I am selling the glass bouquets. I'm applying for a grant. I am working on the *Just Make It (Through)* web comic. I have two others in planning. I want to publish a poem chapbook. I do have some spare poems that are finished. It's getting to that chapbook length. That's been pretty challenging. There are other papers that I've already written and want to publish. I want to learn how to sew specifically to make the most gender-affirming clothing I can and to really figure out how best to express myself in that way.

Reflection: What are your intentions for the future?

What are your intentions for the future? How are you currently creating change? How might you make a difference going forward?

. . . .

. . . .

. . . .

CHAPTER 8
HOLDING THE VISION

What are the actions that you can take to make the world a better place, one that will sustain you as well as the collective?

What would you like to see and not see in the world? Note a few items/experiences that concern you and a few items/experiences which would improve society, make the world a better place and support the planet. Please list your top five items. If you have more than five items, continue in your journal (the possibilities are limitless!). It's okay if you have fewer than five items. These lists are not ranked yet, so just record them in the order they come to mind.

Concerns:

1. ....

2. ....

3. ....

4. ....

5. ....

Improvements! More of this, please:

1. ....

2. ....

3. ....

4. ....

5. ....

Now, circle your top three items from each list.

Of those three, put a star next to your top priority item(s) and re-write them:

Top concern(s): ....

Top improvement(s): ....

Invoking the world of your dreams

Who or what are you holding the vision for?

....

....

Who or what are you honoring as you hold the vision?

....

....

Visioning statements

Say each of the following completed statements aloud. As you say them, you may also want to put your hand on your heart or invoke a feeling of love as you visualize what you want and see it rooted in the earth and surrounded with color (perhaps a rainbow or silver and gold).

Fill in the blank to specify who or what you are sending love and care to. Repeat this template as many times as you like, each time changing what is written in the blank. If you prefer to revise the template, please do! Make it meaningful for you.

Here's to . . . . (particular individuals or groups of people/ animals/etc.) living fully in abundance, health and love and free from fear.

. . . .

. . . .

. . . .

For the next statement, fill in the blank with your ideas from the **Concerns** list. Again, repeat the template multiple times.

Here's to ending:

. . . .

. . . .

. . . .

For the next statement, fill in the blank with the affirmative of what you want. What do you want to see more of? Use your ideas from the **Improvements** list.

Here's to:

....

....

....

End by saying "thank you."

Community circle

Now, let's hear from Alise, Grayson, Helen and Soul about what they **most want to see change** and their **visions for the world.**

Alise

Something that I really want to see change is how people empathize with each other and how they learn about issues. I want to instill so much more empathy and compassion in myself and for myself and in other people so that people are actually willing to delve into these issues and do a lot more work than is being done right now.

People worry so much about public image and about things other than the people that they could be helping. So, that's something that I just really want to see change: people helping and making space for others to lift up their voice. People knowing when to take up space, when to not take up space, being so much more self-aware, so much more empathetic and like the inner workings of social justice.

When I think of what I want the world to be, I just think of the summer programs that I went to. I'm committed to having a world that is always heading towards justice. That's my vision for the world—one where we're constantly questioning our systems. Is this serving everyone? Is this enabling everyone to be active and to participate in society and have a good life? No matter what their origin story is. That is definitely my vision. A world where all of us are committed to making things change, not to having a perfect world, but just wanting things to change. That's what I want to happen.

Grayson

I have many visions for the world. I want people to be able to accept one another without needing explanation. When someone comes to you and trusts you with their identity, there should be no question. There should be no pushback. There should only be acceptance. I think it needs to start with transgender identities being normalized in every setting. We must accept diverse gender identities and expressions, end stigma, and end violence against transgender and gender nonconforming people! It's really important to talk about bathrooms, actually, because people are

always like, "Oh, bathroom talk is uncomfortable." But it's a problem that trans people have to deal with every single day. It's terrifying. For me, in all four years of high school, I tried to use the bathroom maybe twice. And because of that, I have had very bad health impacts. The few times that I have absolutely had to use the bathroom in public, I have had instances of harassment. I just hope that at some point we, as a society, get to the point where it is the norm to have accessible and safe bathrooms for everyone.

Helen

What do I most want to see change? No more landlords—everyone can just live in places, eliminating land ownership as a concept. We would get rid of houselessness by just housing people. There are enough houses to house everyone. Abolishing the prison system, replacing the police force with a team of people who are trained to de-escalate conflict, like mediators, people who are knowledgeable about the legal opportunities  and strategies for undocumented people. Comprehensive sex education that is required to be medically accurate and include things like pleasure, sexually transmitted infections, consent, masturbation, body dysmorphia and conversations about trans things and LGB/queer topics in general. And more non-gendered bathrooms would be useful in public spaces as well as private spaces, because most people have non-gender-specific bathrooms in their private spaces, like their homes. I would also de-criminalize sex work. Abortion would be much more accessible and, in general, women's healthcare services would be expanded, although it's not only women who use those services, and not all women do. And it would be great to get rid of capitalism, but that's perhaps too big a goal. But while I'm at it, you know, throw that one in there, too. [Laughs] Let's hope the world we envision can come to pass.

Soul

I want people to stop saying I'm too young to be disabled. That's the main reason why I shaved my head originally—because of disability speaking type of events

that mattered a lot to me, and I wanted to show that I'm proud of my scars. I think my scars are beautiful. The reason I kept it up is because I got less of that [people saying I'm too young to be disabled]. I still get it, which just kind of blows my mind a bit.

I also want gender markers taken off IDs. There's a ton of other politics like that.

My state has service dog-in-training rights, so I did have the right to take my dog Storm out in public, and he made my life so much better, especially in terms of my physical health. Some service dog waiting lists are eight years long. That's a vision: that people can get the support they need, without going through what I did, without even needing to consider it.

Reflection: Visions for the world

Are you inspired about the visions for the world described by Alise, Grayson, Helen and Soul? Do you share their visions and concerns? Do you have visions they did not mention?

. . . .

. . . .

. . . .

Can you affirm their visions? Social structures that exist now are not all that is possible. There are infinite possibilities. We are creative and powerful! Can you suspend disbelief? Can you help dream these visions into being?

. . . .

. . . .

. . . .

Grayson uses the word "normalize." What does it mean to make something normal? Think about what characteristics have been socially deemed as "other," "abnormal," "not normal," "weird" or "less than." How do we make sure that every identity and every experience is considered "normal," including how we look, who we love, how our brains and bodies function and process, what we do with our bodies (safely/consensually), and every other difference? Please don't accept or normalize hate or hateful policies, laws and practices. Hate keeps people in shame and fear and leaves individuals and communities without needed resources. It creates divides that make it easier to harm someone or many people, even (and sometimes especially) family members and intimate partners.

At the beginning of the chapter, we focused on a vision for the world. Let's revisit that vision with a focus on our heart and body wisdom now. Are you curious to see if there will be a different response? Let's find out! Conduct some body-knowledge research!

Heart-centered visualization

This is an experiment in listening to the heart. If possible, find a quiet, comfortable place for 10–15 minutes. Reduce or remove any distractions (such as phone notifications). You could read through the words, then close your eyes. Another option could be to have someone read the words aloud to you while you relax. You could do the same for the other person or people. You could even record your own voice. If you find yourself so relaxed that you fall asleep, that's okay. Rest well! If there is anything that you are uncomfortable with or at any point you want to stop, just open your eyes and notice yourself in the room. If you try this experiment and find that you are not experiencing anything in particular or are distracted by thoughts, just keep coming back to your heart and your breath. There is no right or wrong experience. It's all an invitation to listen in and become more aware of yourself. You may want to have a pen nearby to record your thoughts afterwards. You could also use colored pencils, markers, paints or other materials.

Let's begin!

Notice your breath. Is your breathing shallow or deep? Is there a feeling of openness or constriction? Whatever is present, just allow it to be. Release judgment. It is just as it is. Now bring your awareness to your heart. Be curious about your heart. How is that precious, beating heart today? Offer your body some love and gratitude. You could say silently or aloud, "Thank you, heart. I am grateful for your energy and flow. I love you, heart."

If you are willing and able, place one hand on your heart area.

Take a few deep breaths to clear and release any tension or thoughts. We are getting curious about what your heart needs. Imagine your heart is a dear friend of yours and you are enjoying its company. Perhaps your heart is expressing an emotion. Whatever it is, just allow it. Thank it for sharing. Can you hear or feel your heart beating or pulsing? Can you feel its aliveness?

Ask your heart, "What do you need right now?"

Pause, breathe and feel as you listen to your heart. Just allow whatever words, images, colors, scents, feelings or other senses you experience. It may feel a bit like a dream. Just accept and receive.

Take a few moments to witness your heart.

When you are ready, ask your heart, "What is your vision for the world?"

Again, just allow whatever comes through to your mind and body without judgment. Notice how you feel.

Take a few moments to allow your heart to express itself.

When you feel complete and your heart has fully expressed itself, offer your love and gratitude to your heart. Thank it for having this visit with you. Know that it is always here for you. All you need to do is place your attention or hand on your heart.

You can conclude this experience by saying silently or aloud, "My heart is always with me. Thank you, heart."

Take a few moments to gently become fully present in the room. Sit quietly. If you would like to take time to record your experience, feel free to do so below or in your personal journal.

Journal: My heart expresses

If you received responses from your heart that you want to record, feel free to write or draw them below or in your personal journal. If you did not receive responses from your heart, imagine what your heart might say.

What does your heart need?

. . . .

. . . .

. . . .

. . . .

. . . .

. . . .

What is your heart's vision for the world?

. . . .

. . . .

. . . .

. . . .

. . . .

. . . .

Express yourself with colored pencils, markers, paints, pastels or any other medium.

Follow-up: What action would you like to take based on your heart's needs or visions? How can you contribute to your "heart world" vision every day?

....

....

....

Flip that script! Encore

Consider statements that represent the current dominant worldview. These may or may not be things you believe. Let's "flip it" to widen our sense of possibility.

Here are two examples of how it works:

1. Valuing competition over collaboration
   Flip it! Valuing collaboration over competition
2. Devaluing femininity, women, girls, and femmes
   Flip it! Valuing femininity, women, girls, and femmes

Now it's your turn. Write the flipped version of each dominant worldview.

Valuing profits over people

Flip it! ....

Valuing profits over stewardship of the Earth

Flip it! ....

Valuing buying things over caring for people and the Earth

Flip it! ....

Devaluing intuition and natural life rhythms

Flip it! . . . .

Valuing "might makes right" over humanity; valuing war over peace

Flip it! . . . .

Valuing the dominant white culture over Black, Brown and Indigenous bodies and lives

Flip it! . . . .

Valuing sameness over difference

Flip it! . . . .

There are so many dominant worldviews. Write a few more and then flip them!

Worldview: . . . .

Flip it! . . . .

Worldview: . . . .

Flip it! . . . .

Worldview: . . . .

Flip it! . . . .

When examples of oppressive thinking present themselves in life, remind yourself and other people to "Flip it!"—reverse it, interrupt it and derail it. Create space for choice and experience. Pause, breathe and feel into your body. How does it feel? What is needed to heal?

Best practices

What are some of the best practices and strategies to create a culture of respect and acceptance? Consent and transformative justice (restorative justice, too)!

Consent is basically asking for and receiving permission. It applies to everyday tasks as well as sexual requests. There are many situations where consent happens or is assumed. Once you start to notice interactions that involve consent, you will see them everywhere. Who is assumed to have power? Who is expected to comply without consenting? Why is that the case? Fostering a "consent culture" means people are encouraged to slow down and pay attention to themselves and each other—to listen to each other and notice body language, to ask for what they want and be empowered to say no or negotiate an alternative. Pay attention and respect what other people want or do not want, and expect respect for all bodies and space. Consent is an everyday action and practice. Only yes means yes. Ambiguous responses are not consent. Ask for what you want. Don't just take something or do something or assume that you are entitled to it. Pressuring someone or taking advantage of someone (and joking about it) is certainly not consent.

Notice and honor your feelings. Practice asserting yourself. **Please seek support if you have a non-consenting experience and you need help.** The Bay Area Transformative Justice Collective offers a process of identifying your support "pod" of people you can turn to in the face of harm/violence, and people you can reach out to when you need to be held accountable.[1] Alise shares that this resource has been a useful framework for her and her friends.

Did you consent to participate in patriarchy, white supremacy or any other interlocking system of oppression? Uh, probably not. Would you agree to it if you were consented? Let's actively work towards building systems to which we can say yes!

Helen's vision for society includes "Abolishing the prison system, replacing the police force with a team of people who are trained to de-escalate conflict..." This is part of a big idea about transforming society by eliminating the Prison Industrial Complex. Community organizers have been working tirelessly to hold space for transformative justice and to promote it as a model practice. What is transformative justice? How is it different from restorative justice? How can we build a culture of consent, repair and transformation?

Restorative justice repairs hurt and harm in a way that respects all parties' feelings, needs and dignity. It includes individuals taking responsibility, problem-solving and accountability to the community (in schools, the community is the student body). The process is about making things right in relationships, not about punishment. It involves listening, empathy and perspective-taking to recognize the impact of one's behavior on another person or group of people, and taking action to repair it.

Transformative justice includes all of the restorative justice elements and goes to the root of the issue at a systemic level to transform the conditions that caused the harm. Disability justice and transformative justice writer, educator and trainer Mia Mingus shares some key elements of transformative justice, such as supporting survivors, helping harm-doers and community members take accountability, and fostering support and skill-building for interventions in the community including violence interruption and prevention.[2]

How do we take responsibility for harms we have committed? We can start by apologizing.

Practice responding: Apologizing

When I was a classroom teacher and needed to understand a situation further to help resolve a conflict, I would ask the student(s) three questions:

1. What happened?
2. Why did it happen?
3. What will you do differently in the future?

Let's use that three-question framework as we consider responding to someone we have hurt in regard to systemic oppression (or for general situations). Please adapt the apology to make it your own and in your authentic voice. This framework can also be used when you want to experience what receiving an apology would sound like. You can say it to yourself or have a third party read it to you on behalf of the person or institution from whom/which you would want to hear it.

Sample apology

I apologize. I recognize how I violated your trust by carelessly using racist language. I was disrespectful. I commit to taking steps to learn more about how white supremacy operates so I can do better going forward. I know trust takes time to rebuild. Please know that I am ready to listen if and when you want to talk about how I hurt you. I will not interrupt you, argue with you or minimize the impact of my behavior. I take responsibility for the harm I caused. I will be more self-reflective going forward. Thank you for receiving my apology. Please let me know if there is anything I can do to repair our relationship.

Break it down

In the sample apology:

1. Underline "What happened?"
2. Put a circle around "Why/how did it happen?"
3. Place stars/asterisks at the beginning and end of "What will you do differently in the future?"
4. Place parentheses/brackets around "What system(s) of oppression is/are at play?"

That last question is added for emphasis to help us recognize the big picture. The question of "why" is not really addressed, so just focus on "how it happened."

Answer key for "Break it down"

If you have different responses, that's okay!

1. What happened? (underlined): I violated your trust
2. Why/how did it happen? (circled): carelessly using racist language
3. What will you do differently in the future? (stars/asterisks): taking steps to learn more about how white supremacy operates; be more self-reflective going forward
4. What system(s) of oppression is/are at play? (parenthesis/brackets): racism/white supremacy

Taking responsibility by offering an apology

The next four prompts are useful for you to consider as you craft your own apology.[3] Check any items which apply in your situation (✓). Use them in place of the items in the sample apology.

1. **What happened?** I/we:

   ❑ acted in an insensitive way ❑ hurt your feelings

   ❑ caused physical harm ❑ violated your trust

Write in: ....

2. **Why/how did it happen?** Add your own details.

   ❑ Acting aggressively towards you ❑ Denying your experience

   ❑ Disrespecting

   ❑ Assuming ❑ Excluding

   ❑ Blaming ❑ Expressing biased attitudes

   ❑ Deceiving ❑ Exploiting

- ❏ Gossiping
- ❏ Harassing
- ❏ Ignoring/neglecting
- ❏ Insulting
- ❏ Judging
- ❏ Lying
- ❏ Misgendering repeatedly
- ❏ Mocking and/or telling insensitive "jokes"
- ❏ Not listening

- ❏ Not respecting boundaries
- ❏ Shaming
- ❏ Stereotyping
- ❏ Touching without consent
- ❏ Using offensive language
- ❏ Violating confidentiality by sharing personal business that was not mine to share
- ❏ Withholding information/ resources

Write in: ....

3. **What will you do differently in the future?** What is the remedy (learning/behavior change, systemic change) that is needed? Write your own response:

....

....

....

4. **What system(s) of oppression is/are at play?**

....

....

....

Use this space to write your own apology. Keep the focus on the person/people who you hurt. Avoid centering yourself (such as "I had good intentions") during the apology.

· ·

· ·

· ·

Who do you intend to share this apology with? When might you offer it? What do you hope will happen? Consider best-case, worst-case and middle-ground options. Are you okay with any outcome? Connect with people in your support network/pod as needed.

· ·

· ·

· ·

What helps? What hurts?

Let's think about helpful forces for empowerment, transformation and liberation and compare them to harmful oppressive forces.

Directions: In this activity, there are two category headings: **Helping** and **Harming**. Match each numbered Helping item in the left column with its **opposite** Harming item in the right column. There are many possibilities for what might be considered opposites. Some items do not have an exact opposite. The letters of the Harming items are intended to be both capital letters and lower-case letters. When all of your letter answers are filled in, read down the column for a message!

Helping	Harming
1. Acceptance, inclusion	A. War
2. Body wisdom and care	a. Oppressive practices, destruction of life
3. Care for the planet/environment	d. Hate, misery
4. Community/collective focus (unity consciousness)	E. Rejection, exclusion
5. Consent	e. Disrespect or dismissal of cultural differences
6. Cultural humility and respect of culture	F. Profit-driven greed (prioritize profits over people)
7. Equality, equity, justice	M. Disregard, exploitation and brutality towards people, animals, nature
8. Healing/liberation practices	m. Disregard of the body, bodily harm, body only attended to when there is an issue
9. Acknowledging history	N. Excess for some, lack for others
10. Love, laughter, joy, whimsy, magic	n. Ignoring, revising, silencing or dismissing history
11. Listening	O. Business as usual (harms unrepaired and perpetuated)
12. Mutual support, interdependence	o. Individualism
13. Peace	p. Destruction of the planet/ environment for profit/progress/ productivity
14. People have enough of what they need	R. Offering support out of pity, disconnection
15. Power from within, self-determination	R. Withholding resources
16. Prioritize people over profits	r. Superiority/inferiority, inequality, injustice

....	17. Reparations (repair/remedy harms)	S. Power/domination/control over the bodies and lives of other people
....	18. Sharing resources	T. Refusal to listen, silencing
....	19. Value and respect life, dignity	w. Force, coercion, intimidation

Are there any **Helping** items that are missing from the list? If so, write them here:

. . . .

. . . .

. . . .

Are there any items that could be considered **both** Helping and Harming? If so, list them here and describe the situation.

. . . .

. . . .

. . . .

Answer key for "What helps? What hurts?"

There are other ways to arrange this list, so please don't worry if your pairs are different!

1. E 2. m 3. p 4. o 5. w 6. e 7. r 8. a 9. n 10. d 11. T 12. R 13. A

14. N 15. S 16. F 17. O 18. R 19. M

Message: Empower and TRANSFORM

Why transform? So that we can create a society and world in which every person has the resources and support they need to thrive, achieve their purpose and potential, and no one is regarded as expendable or less than.

Why is it important to understand the difference between Helping and Harming forces? On our life journeys, we will encounter a variety of experiences. It's useful to recognize the forces as they show up. Ask yourself, "Is this a force of help or harm?" In addition, we will use Helping forces as we craft our project in Chapter 10. In preparation, please re-read the list of Helping forces (the numbered items on the left side in the activity). Put a star/asterisk (*) next to your favorite concepts. Next, write your top five favorites here and briefly describe why each is important to you or how you apply it in your life.

My top five favorite Helping forces

1. ....

2. ....

3. ....

4. ....

5. ....

Creating the House of Transformation/Liberation

Let's create a sculpture of a house to represent building a more just and equitable world. This is what you will need:

Something to build with: Use whatever materials you have around the house or in nature, such as cardboard, sticks, clay, blocks, toothpicks, buttons, stones, coins, index cards, folded paper, wire hanger, or fabric.

Something to write with: Pencil, pen, marker, or crayon.

Optional: Scissors, glue/tape/string, paint, glitter, stickers, or other decorations.

Before or after you sculpt/create, if it is possible to write on your building material, please do! If not, write on paper or fabric and attach it to your creation. Write words or phrases that represent liberation such as healing, repair, dignity, justice, freedom, compassion, care, resources and abundance. Write phrases such as Black Lives Matter, Indigenous Sovereignty, Queer Liberation, Trans Justice, Disability Justice, Women's Rights, Workers' Rights, BIPOC Queer and Trans Lives Matter, and so on. Write what you want to see and build. You may want to refer back to the previous activity about helping forces.

Build your sculpture. It can be as intricate or as elaborate as you would like. It can be four "walls" only or a more elaborate structure or it might just be a representation. It does not have to look a certain way. It's up to you. Express yourself and allow your creation to take shape without judgment.

How do you build a new house? You have the power! You are the architect. You are the builder. Your energy, vision and skills are needed in this endeavor.

Name your creation. Call it the **House of Transformation** or the **House of Liberation** or a name that has meaning for you personally or culturally. This is a representation you will keep as a symbol of what is possible. Take your time with this creation. Infuse it with your love, hopes and dreams. Breathe into your intention and our collective intention to create a society that truly cares for all its people. Create from your heart and your higher purpose for the greatest and highest good of all. Enjoy the process. When it is complete, look with love at your creation. Release fear and judgment. It is perfectly imperfect. Relax and enjoy what you made. Admire it and look at it from different perspectives.

Pause and breathe mindfully to experience how your body feels in this moment. Is there a sense of peacefulness or excitement? Are there any sensations? Where?

Please record what you notice here or in your journal:

. . . .

. . . .

. . . .

Remember, humans built systems of domination and injustice. Humans created racism and racist policies. Humans created gender roles and the gender binary and all other mechanisms of oppression and inequity. Humans can change these structures. Humans—specifically you—can become more aware of the game that is being played and refuse to play by those rules. It is possible and we have the collective power and vision to make it happen, especially when we join forces!

Thank you for holding the vision and co-creating the new ways of society. I am excited to see the developments!

CHAPTER 9
ACTION AND SUSTAINING THE MOMENTUM

Alise, Grayson, Helen and Soul discuss the **actions** they take to make a difference. They all reference the Diversity Trainers, so let's learn about that model project first!

Model project: Diversity Trainers

The Diversity Trainers are a group of high school students who lead sensitivity training for each other and middle school students. I had the honor of being the faculty sponsor of this project for nearly 20 years. The magic of this group is love, listening, willingness to learn and to educate, authenticity and vulnerable sharing. Students share stories and what matters most to them, illuminating the social issues they face to foster empathy and ally action. Diversity Trainers focus on what actions students can take in their everyday lives: listen, learn more, care, accept people, speak/stand up for justice (including in class conversations), interrupt bullying and bias incidents, and challenge assumptions and systems.

High school students bring their skills, creativity and leadership to the group to design and develop new activities and conversation starters which educate, broaden perspectives and deepen community connections. In middle school classrooms, high school students help their younger peers recognize the signs and symptoms of interpersonal and structural inequality.

Confidentiality and empathy are key elements of the group. There are student-led presentations, listening panels and workshops in which student leaders create sessions on the subjects that are most meaningful to them, including: intersectionality, neurodiversity, disabilities, mental health, racism, feminism, sexism, gender beyond the binary, sexuality, Islamaphobia, anti-Semitism, and immigration issues. There are also sessions led by guest presenters focusing on topics ranging from civil rights activism to grief and grieving, non-violent communication, LGBTQ+ issues and so much more. Diversity Trainers create a space of belonging and a culture of acceptance in which students are encouraged to be fully themselves and listen to and learn from each other. It has a positive ripple effect on the school and district.

Now, let's enjoy learning about the **actions** Alise, Grayson, Helen and Soul take to make a difference.

Alise

In the first half of my high school career, Diversity Trainers was a big way that I explored activism. I felt just so empowered doing Diversity Trainers, going to the night meetings, learning so much and being in community with other people who really did care as much as I did. It was super gratifying for me. I loved creating the Racism Hazards game and the racism workshop. I did that with my twin sister Alana and  a couple of other student leaders. It was so much fun creating that slideshow with them because we all just vibed while we were tackling really heavy stuff. It was just nice being in community with them, having humor and even with these really hard-hitting topics, being able to relate to each other.

I had grown up among white friends all my life. I was realizing there were these differences between us that they didn't really understand and I was having to explain myself. I was figuring out what actions I actually did want to take that weren't exhausting to me, and that made me feel I was really making a difference and not just making myself feel horrible. I found a lot of that in writing. I went to a couple of protests. My actions have been more about what I can do locally for people I know and for people I really love and care about. Throughout high school, my friends became more diverse. Being able to be there for them in struggles that are institutional-related, and having compassion for the people I love and who are there for me is a big part of my action. I also advocated for a Pan-African Studies course, which ended up running in my senior year.

Grayson

I began my action path with educating through the GSA sophomore health class presentations, which I started during my freshman year and have done every semester since (besides the spring 2020 semester when we were online). That really fueled my passion because when I got into those classrooms and I started talking about different identities within the LGBTQ+ community, many people had no idea what I was talking about and they genuinely wanted to learn. People really started to listen when they realized that it was not just the GSA kids who knew about this stuff. When there were other kids in the classroom who said, "Yes, I know what genderqueer means. I know what intersex means," that was another method of breaking the stigma that I found. It was incredibly helpful. I realized from that point on that if I have my platform, then people will listen. Since then, I've just been building my platform and sharing more education and personal experiences. I made a presentation to the Diversity Trainers when I was in tenth grade. I got to speak to a hundred of my peers about how to be an ally to trans students. That really showed me that I could use my voice. I have suffered with extreme social anxiety since I was in eighth grade. Working through my fears and the things that gave me such immense anxiety has only shown me just how much more powerful I can be than I thought. The biggest presentation I've done now has been for 250 doctors. It's incredibly liberating knowing that I used to be someone who needed a doctor's note to get excused from class presentations to 20 people, and now I stand on a stage and am broadcasted on the internet and speak to doctors and other people. It's a great feeling. I'm so glad that I've had these opportunities.

Grayson at the mic!

Helen

When I was in high school, one of my plays was produced for the Diversity Trainers Conference of that year. My play, a light-hearted comedy, was about some issues that felt relevant for that conference so it was a really cool way of doing activism through art by having it produced. The play had gender nonconforming characters, queer relationships, and discussion of bisexual erasure, femme-phobia, and the social gap that

can arise between people in the queer community (even just as allies) and those who have no relationships with queer people as they try to connect.

I designed a few activities for Diversity Trainers in high school. I made one activity about assumptions we make when not given many identifiers, called "The Neutral Story." That was basically a short story we would read out loud to students and then ask them to tell us about the characters. While none of the characters was explicitly male or white or non-disabled and so on, the students would usually assume they were. That gave us the opportunity to look closer at that trend and encourage students to be aware of those assumptions.

One activity I'm really proud of was a training packet I made with Soul about slurs, providing the history and context of a word and offering suggestions for better, non-hurtful words to use instead. I think a lot of people use dehumanizing language, not because they're cruel and trying to be mean, but because they don't realize that it has the background that it has, and that it could hurt the people around them. I've had a number of occasions in college where I've had to inform people by saying, "Hey, I know you definitely didn't mean to do/say this in a hurtful way. But just so you know, this is the background on that and people who are from this community have asked that we do not use that language."

I created another activity about intersectionality and how different forms of oppression affect people differently. "Rules of the Game" revealed how different mechanics and structures of oppression are interlocking and can hurt people who are more vulnerable and have more identities that are marginalized in ways that people who don't have those identities are completely unaware of or don't notice.

Soul

In high school, Diversity Trainers, like so much of my action, was just work that I felt compelled to do. Nothing gave me greater meaning at that time in my life than being a part of Diversity Trainers. So I wouldn't have missed a meeting for the world. There were things I did in the past and then my health started to fail and I couldn't continue to attend protests. I spoke at my university for

a panel about art and disability and the intersection thereof. I was invited by Disability Services. At the time, I had my service dog Storm with me. I find trans communities online and trans people who need support, who have questions, and I talk them through mental health care and gender-affirming surgeries; like if you have a doctor, email them, email their staff, here's a template for the letter that you can send your insurance, here are the next steps. It's also about providing support when they're like, "My family really sucks," and just being there for them.

Reflection: Making a difference

Were you surprised by any of the ways of making a difference the interviewees described? Were you inspired by them? Do you take any similar actions?

. . . .

. . . .

. . . .

Let's keep thinking about actions to take by reflecting on gender roles.

Patriarchy's penalties

This activity was inspired by Helen's "Rules of the Game" for the Diversity Trainers.[1]

Stereotypes are described in this activity so that we may bring an awareness to how they are at play and why they persist, not because they are valid. Stereotypes and expectations vary by racialization, social class, gender, culture and other factors.

Who are the following stereotypes, assumptions and expectations directed towards?

A Transgender girls	E Transgender boys	I Non-binary people
B Cisgender girls	F Cisgender boys	J People of other genders
C Transgender women	G Transgender men	K Femme men
D Cisgender women	H Cisgender men	L Butch women

Who does this apply to? Write the letter choice(s) (multiple correct answers)	#	Stereotypes, assumptions and expectations
	1.	Expected to be nice, sweet and/or quiet
	2.	Expected to be in control
	3.	Dismissed as overly emotional or sensitive
	4.	Expected not to show emotions
	5.	Excessive emphasis on personal appearance
	6.	Vulnerable when out alone
	7.	Questioned/hassled in public restrooms or locker rooms
	8.	Assumed to be "confused" or that "It's a phase"
	9.	Assumed to be assertive/aggressive
	10.	Expected to "need a man"
	11.	Assumed to be "too young to know"
	12.	Sexually harassed or touched without consent
	13.	Assumed to be gay/lesbian/queer
	14.	Held to unrealistic beauty standards

cont.

Who does this apply to? Write the letter choice(s) (multiple correct answers)	#	Stereotypes, assumptions and expectations
	15.	Receive unsolicited advice about personal appearance
	16.	Expected to reject things that are "for girls" or "feminine"

Answer key for **"Patriarchy's penalties"**

Please note: There are many possible responses for each item. If your response is not listed, consider it correct as well.

1. A–D, K
2. E–H, L
3. A–D, K
4. E–H, L
5. A–D
6. A–D, E, G, I–L

7. A, C, E, G, I, J
8. A, C, E, G, I, J
9. E–H, L
10. D
11. A, E, I, J
12. A–D, K

13. K, L
14. A–D
15. A–D, E, G
16. E–H

What action can you take?

Given the harms of gender stereotypes, assumptions and expectations, how can you proceed?

1. Become aware of and identify stereotypes about how people are "supposed to" behave according to gender roles (or any other socially determined expectations).
2. Notice when these messages play in your mind and the effect they have on your behavior. Use "The shame and stigma shut down" activity as needed.
3. Decide how you want to relate to gender role expectations (accept, refuse, resist, subvert).
4. Interrupt stereotypes, prejudice and discrimination.
5. Build relationships based on authenticity. Embrace strength and vulnerability in all people.

6. Speak up about the harmful effects of gender expectations (on everyone).
7. Help others to identify stereotypes and move beyond them.
8. Work towards creating equitable and inclusive policies, practices, and cultures.
9. What other actions can you take?

. . . .

. . . .

. . . .

Debunking the myth of "reverse racism"

Why do some people think saying Black Lives Matter is "racist against white people"? Are attempts to remedy current and historic discrimination against Black, Brown and Indigenous people "reverse racism"? Let's consider which groups of people are being marginalized or harmed by a variety of policies and practices. This is not easy or light content. Proceed with care and know that it is important to witness if you have the capacity to do so.

Check (✓) the column that best represents the GROUP of people who have/had these kinds of experiences. BIPOC stands for Black, Indigenous and people of color. Consider white people the set of people who have advantages based on skin color in the United States, not particular ethnic or nationality groups.

BIPOC	White people	Which GROUP has/had this experience in the United States?
		Made fun of because of physical features (skin, hair, face, body) and subjected to persistent dehumanizing stereotypes
		Little or no positive representation in politics and mass media (movies, television, radio, advertising)

cont.

BIPOC	White people	Which GROUP has/had this experience in the United States?
		Excluded from jobs, neighborhoods, schools and voting
		Earn significantly less money than their counterparts for the same jobs (called the "wage gap")
		Forcibly relocated from their homes and land
		Their children taken away without their consent (stolen) never to be seen again or put into schools to "unlearn" their language or culture
		Targeted for violence and hatred for the color of their skin or culture
		Terrorized by an organized hate group
		Given harsher sentences when accused of a crime
		Disproportionately high rates of imprisonment (mass incarceration)
		Crimes perpetrated against them and their communities go unpunished and socially sanctioned
		Limited in access to clean water, fresh food, sanitation or other essential resources
		Exposed to unhealthful conditions in schools (lead paint, asbestos, etc.) and/or in neighborhoods (trash/waste processing, unregulated manufacturing or utility hazards, etc.)
		Disproportionately higher rates of disease and infant mortality (death) and shorter life expectancy (earlier death) compared to the general population
		Cultural artifacts and treasures stolen and displayed by the dominant culture
		Limited access to culturally sensitive and responsive medical and/or mental/behavioral healthcare
		Fewer rights, or considered less than full citizens or subject to unjust laws (such as Jim Crow Laws and Black Codes)
		The target of racial profiling

		Considered exotic
		Placed in internment camps and/or have/had their children locked in cages; mass deportation
		Held captive or enslaved and forced to labor for no compensation
		Their history erased or revised by the dominant culture
		Lower expectations of achievement from teachers and society
		Dismissed, silenced, told to "get over it" and physically harmed when raising concerns of mistreatment and injustice

The list goes on and on and there is so much more than what is listed here. Unfortunately.

If white people as a group were being consistently and persistently harmed in these ways over years and generations, perhaps there might be a shred of truth in the claim of systemic "reverse racism." It is BIPOC as a group who have had these experiences of systemic injustice for generations. White people as a group have not been subjected to these constant indignities, disadvantages and atrocities in the United States (and who is considered white is an ongoing process of racialization). Historically and currently in the U.S., white people are the overwhelming majority in power in the government, business, schools, banking, housing, healthcare, law enforcement and the media. It is a protection mechanism of white supremacy to deflect blame away from itself. White author, facilitator and professor Robin DiAngelo, Ph.D., calls this defensive strategy "white fragility" and describes it as form of bullying in which white people feel victimized, attacked, silenced, shamed, blamed, accused, insulted and outraged around any racial challenges and exhibit behaviors such as crying, arguing, denying, avoiding and/or leaving.[2] She explains: "White equilibrium is a cocoon of racial comfort, centrality, superiority, entitlement, racial apathy, and obliviousness, all rooted in an identity of being good people free of racism."[3] Claiming "reverse racism" is an example of white fragility/supremacy. It is a tactic (intentional or unconscious) designed to keep power in the hands of white people.

Author, speaker and podcast host Layla F. Saad describes in detail the effects and indicators of white supremacy and guides readers to unpack their own experiences with privilege and power in *Me and White Supremacy: Combat Racism, Change the World, and Become a Good Ancestor*.[4] Saad clarifies the difference between prejudice (held by an individual) and racism (which operates as a system) and reminds us that when white people are not centered, they often feel marginalized, which leads to white fragility responses. Saad helps readers understand aspects and nuances of anti-Blackness, racial stereotypes, cultural appropriation and how we can all work towards dismantling white supremacy within ourselves and society.

One way white supremacy operates is to revise, deny and silence history. Injustices from the past must be taught and understood in their full depth and breadth, not glossed over, not replaced with myths. There needs to be a personal and collective reckoning, including public recognition and repair/reparations for slavery and genocide in the form of public apologies, financial compensation and returning land back to Indigenous peoples.

In 2008, the U.S. House of Representatives apologized to African Americans "for the wrongs committed against them and their ancestors who suffered under slavery and Jim Crow" and expressed "its commitment to rectify the lingering consequences of the misdeeds...and to stop the occurrence of human rights violations in the future."[5] However, there was no financial compensation for 250 years of stolen labor, and an additional 150 years of injustice, and we continue to see ongoing human rights violations.

The Electoral Justice Project of the Movement for Black Lives created the BREATHE Act to support reparations and invest in community development and safety using federal funds divested from policing and imprisonment. The goal is to create "sustainable and equitable communities for all people," hold officials accountable and enhance the "self-determination of Black communities."[6]

Indigenous organizers are calling for lands that were taken by colonial settlers and the U.S. government to be returned to Indigenous peoples. "The movement goes beyond the transfer of deeds to include respecting Indigenous rights, preserving languages and traditions, and ensuring food sovereignty, housing, and clean air and water."[7] All of these rights are upheld by the United Nations Declaration on the Rights of Indigenous Peoples.[8] Krystal Two Bulls (Oglala Lakota and Northern Cheyenne), Director of the Landback campaign with NDN Collective, emphasizes returning lands to Indigenous stewardship as well as dismantling white supremacy and defunding "all of the mechanisms that enforce white supremacy—the military-industrial complex, the police, ICE, border patrol."[9] [ICE = U.S. Immigration and Customs Enforcement]

What is the history of the land on which you live? How can we acknowledge the harms done and offer reparations towards justice?

What actions can we take to bring about reparations?

. . . .

. . . .

. . . .

Earth lover

Can you pause now to get outside and connect with the Earth? If possible, touch the ground with your hands or feet or whole body. Did you ever lie on your back and look up at the stars? Take a nature walk or hike? Sit on a rock or under a tree? Try that now. See if you can get quiet within yourself and just feel connected. It can be just for a minute or for as long as you want. Notice everything you can while you are outside. What do you see, hear, smell, taste and touch from above, below and all around you? How do you feel within yourself?

There are lots of ways to connect with the Earth if you are in a space without direct access. Hold a plant or a crystal or a shell. Feel grounded and rooted to the Earth when you eat vegetables grown underground like carrots, beets, onions, garlic and potatoes. Connect with any wood or metal elements. Feel the piece of the Earth you hold and give it love and gratitude.

When you come in from outside or finish connecting with your Earth element, reflect on the following questions.

How is your relationship with the Earth? Is it one-sided? Do we expect the planet to keep on giving while we continuously receive? How can we honor and give back to the Earth? Can we cultivate a more reciprocal relationship with the Earth? Can we offer gratitude, send our planet good wishes and heartfelt energy for healing as we would for others we care about? Can we learn about sustainable practices and put them into effect and encourage others to do the same? Can we support the Indigenous water protectors and land defenders? Can we support policies that create responsible stewardship of the planet and end destructive practices? What are the ways you honor the Earth and take action on behalf of our planet?

. . . .

. . . .

. . . .

CHAPTER 10
MAKE A DIFFERENCE WITH YOUR LOVE IN ACTION!

Here we are! This is it! The culminating chapter where you develop your action plan and the project through which you will make a difference! So exciting! Have fun braiding your ideas, interests, skills and passions into a gorgeous creation.

My social justice commitments

Here are some social justice commitments arranged alphabetically. Many others are possible! Please write in other ideas at the end or throughout this list. Put a check mark in the box (✓) for as many commitments as you want to make! Think about specifics when possible. How will you take action to honor your commitments?

   I commit to:

   ❏   Acknowledging and apologizing when I mess up; learning from my mistakes; committing to doing better

❏   Acknowledging the Indigenous peoples on whose land I
     currently live

❏   Allowing myself to grieve as needed

❏   Amplifying and boosting the voices of people with lived experience
     of oppression

❏   Being fully myself (accepting myself, expressing myself)

❏   Building systems that truly serve all people in policy and practice

❏   Caring for the Earth and all of the inhabitants of the Earth

❏   Celebrating accomplishments

❏   Centering voices of the most vulnerable (this may mean de-
     centering yourself)

❏   Challenging discriminatory laws, policies and practices

❏   Challenging oppression when I hear/see/experience it

❏   Challenging stereotypes

❏   Checking my privilege, levering my privilege

❏   Collaborating/conspiring towards justice with people of lived
     experience of injustice

❏   Continually recommitting myself towards social justice

❏   Creating action networks with inclusive, equitable and
     responsive cultures

❏   Creating and celebrating community

❏   Disrupting and dismantling policies and systems that cause harm
     and do not serve all people

❏   Diversifying my crew (as Alise says)

- ❏ Diversifying my media consumption (seeing empowered people with bodies and identities beyond the dominant culture's beauty standards, as Helen says)

- ❏ Divesting from systems that cause harm

- ❏ Educating myself and others about current and historical injustice and resistance and ways to make a difference

- ❏ Encouraging myself and others to keep taking action towards justice and liberation

- ❏ Exploring my unconscious bias; unpacking it; making a conscious choice to notice my biased thinking and question where it comes from and if it is serving my good and the good of all; releasing what does not serve, replacing it with humanizing stories and truths

- ❏ Exposing the roots of injustice

- ❏ Expressing gratitude

- ❏ Expressing myself creatively (art, dance/movement, etc.)

- ❏ Helping create a society that is "moving in the direction of justice" (as Alise says)

- ❏ Holding the vision of empowerment, justice and liberation for all

- ❏ Honoring the humanity and multi-dimensional aspects of all people

- ❏ Honoring those doing the work and those who came before us

- ❏ Initiating conversations with others around social justice issues

- ❏ Interrupting bias incidents (insensitive jokes, comments, slurs, microaggressions/abuse)

- ❏ Leading with love (even if that love sounds fierce)

- ❏ Learning about and respecting other people's/culture's experiences

- ❏ Learning about the effects of trauma and keeping a trauma-/resilience-informed perspective

❏ Learning from history (Is it a "broken system" or was it designed to benefit some and harm others? What is the history of resistance? Can the system be changed? Are reforms effective?)

❏ Lifelong learning about social issues, acceptance and equity

❏ Living in a sustainable way (for my body and the planet)

❏ Living in an embodied way (being in my body)

❏ Looking at oppression from a policy/systemic perspective (What systems are at play and how do they operate?)

❏ Looking at the harsh reality of injustice; not looking away because it is inconvenient or uncomfortable

❏ Loving myself and others

❏ Overcoming discomfort and fear

❏ Practicing cultural humility (Be humble. Listen.)

❏ Practicing mindfulness

❏ Practicing self-care

❏ Questioning systems (Who is being served/harmed?)

❏ Questioning the dominant culture (Why is any culture dominant? Who benefits/profits?)

❏ Respecting people's self-determination

❏ Sharing my experiences

❏ Speaking up/out and standing up for social justice

❏ Spending time in nature

❏ Supporting action networks or movements led by people with lived experience (financially and/or with time/energy/resources)

❏ Supporting people I know and care about

❏ Supporting equitable and inclusive policies and practices

❏ Taking action towards justice (How? Specify: . . . .)

❏ Telling people how you notice them making a difference

❏ Thinking critically

❏ Upholding dignity and recognizing the humanity of individuals and groups of people

❏ Using my platform and network to educate towards social justice

❏ Working towards the creation and implementation of equitable and inclusive policies and practices

Write in:

. . . .

. . . .

. . . .

Wow! That's a lot! It's all important. What are your most essential commitments? Review the items you checked on the commitments list. Place a star/asterisk (*) next to your top ten priorities. Next, transfer those ten items below (in your own words if possible). The items can be arranged in order of importance but they do not need to be.

1. . . . .

2. . . . .

3. . . . .

4. . . . .

5. ....

6. ....

7. ....

8. ....

9. ....

10. ....

Now, narrow down your top ten list to a top three! Put a circle or diamond around the most essential items from your top ten list. Re-write your top three social justice commitments here:

1. ....

2. ....

3. ....

Great work! You have just identified your top three social justice commitments. That's fantastic!

How often will you check in about your commitments to see if your priorities have shifted?

❏ Daily

❏ Weekly

❏ Every other week

❏ Monthly

❏ Quarterly (every three months)

❏   Annually

❏   Some other interval (specify how often): . . . .

When you re-evaluate your priorities, let it be a special time. Perhaps enjoy some quiet moments or play your favorite music, read some inspirational words or light a candle. Consider doing a heart-centered body awareness practice or visualization. Re-read the original list of commitments and see if your top ten items have changed. Reconsider your top three. It's totally fine to change your priorities and strategies!

Will you have an accountability buddy or group to help you stay focused on actively engaging with your commitments? If yes, who (or what group)? Will you also help that person or group of people keep focused on their commitments? Can your person/group work towards creating a more equitable culture?

. . . .

. . . .

. . . .

Write three ways that you can sustain the momentum of taking action:

1.   . . . .

2.   . . . .

3.   . . . .

Make it intergenerational!

This book is an example of an intergenerational project. It features voices of younger people and older people. People of all ages have wisdom and perspective. Can you think of ways to bring together people of various ages in your project? **Y**ounger and **O**lder **U**nited is an acrostic for YOU and that includes you!

Make it accessible and inclusive!

Remember to consider and prioritize accessibility in your initial planning and throughout your process for your project/event.[1] What are the physical barriers? What attitudes are barriers? Here are some considerations to get you started on thinking about how to make your offering as inclusive as possible. Check items for which arrangements are being made (✓).

❑   Is the physical access to the space barrier-free? Are there curb cuts, accessible entry doors, ramped entrances, elevators, lifts, any stairs?

❑   Are there gender-neutral bathrooms with accessible bathroom stalls (large enough for a wheelchair user and another person)?

❑   Is there ample designated accessible parking? Is it close to the entrance? Is public transportation in close proximity to the venue or will an accessible van/bus be provided?

❑   Is the width of aisles at least 3 feet? Is there reserved seating for people with disabilities and their friends/family/companions? Is there wide seating?

❑   For presentations, will there be (circle all that apply): captioned media, transcription, American Sign Language (ASL) interpretation, other language interpretation, readers, audio descriptions, use of assistive listening devices, telecommunication devices, note takers, color contrast of presentations, plain ("sans serif") font, alternative text used to describe images, topics lists and content warnings, alternative formats (large font size, Braille, or plain language with images) and/or materials provided in advance?

❏   Will there be service dog space, scent-/chemical-free space, lighting considerations, decompression and/or quiet spaces?

❏   Will technology access be considered as well as proficiency with technology? Will there be a technology support service?

❏   Are food options in accessible locations in close proximity? If food is being served, will allergies and dietary restrictions be considered?

❏   Is there financial accessibility? Will there be a sliding scale starting at $0 (with no questions asked), voluntary or suggested donations? Will presenters be paid? Prioritize paying people from historically marginalized and underinvested communities; avoid expecting free labor or resources.

❏   Will there be consideration for mental health needs before, during and after the project/event?

❏   Is there cultural inclusivity through leadership by and representation at all levels of people with disabilities, BIPOC, LGBTQ+ people and people from the culture(s) who will participate? Have you confirmed that your project/event does not conflict with cultural or religious celebrations? How are people from various geographical locations included? People of all ages and sizes?

❏   Will there be training provided for project/event leaders on inclusive/accessible language and etiquette? Is there a designated person for accessibility? Is there a non-discrimination statement or statement of inclusivity? Is it clear how participants make accessibility requests (and by what date) and how to address accessibility concerns?

❏   Are there emergency plans and contingency plans in place? (medics, evacuation plan: clear signage, visual as well as audible signals, emergency lighting, alternatives to lifts and elevators? Protest buddy/arrest plans?) Is there a conflict resolution process? De-escalation training and space? "Know Your Rights" training?

❑   How will you communicate in advance to potential participants so they will be aware of accessibility offerings and can make additional requests?

Review the Americans with Disabilities Act[2] for more detail!

My action plan template

Now is the time to consider your skills, commitments, interests, how you intend to direct your efforts and towards what end, through what process and actions, and through which of your strengths/interests. This information gathering will help you get a clearer sense about your social justice project.

What are your skills?
Check as many as apply (✓):

I am (a/an):

❑   Accepting

❑   Adaptable

❑   Advocator

❑   Aggressive

❑   Analytical

❑   Artistic

❑   Assertive

❑   Authentic

❑   Aware

❑   Brainstormer

❑   Calm in challenging situations

❑   Caring

❑   Collaborative

❑   Committed

❑   Communicator

❑   Compassionate

❑   Confident

❑   Conflict mediator (de-escalator)

❑   Confrontational

❑   Conversation generator (get people talking and thinking)

❑   Cooperative

❑   Coordinator

❑   Courageous

❑   Creative

❑   Critical

❑   Curious

❑   Dancer

❑   Data collector, analyzer and communicator

- ❏ Decision maker
- ❏ Dedicated
- ❏ Delegator
- ❏ Dependable
- ❏ Designer
- ❏ Determined
- ❏ Devoted
- ❏ Diplomatic
- ❏ Dreamer
- ❏ Educator
- ❏ Empathetic
- ❏ Encouraging
- ❏ Experimenter
- ❏ Focused
- ❏ Hardworking
- ❏ Humble
- ❏ Humorous
- ❏ Idea generator
- ❏ Initiator
- ❏ Innovator
- ❏ Insightful
- ❏ Inspired/ inspiring

- ❏ Interpersonal (skills for collaboration)
- ❏ Interpreter (speak/sign language(s))
- ❏ Introspective
- ❏ Intuitive
- ❏ Leader
- ❏ Listener
- ❏ Logical
- ❏ Loyal
- ❏ Magical
- ❏ Motivated
- ❏ Musical
- ❏ Negotiator
- ❏ Networker
- ❏ Observant
- ❏ Open-minded
- ❏ Optimistic
- ❏ Organized
- ❏ Passionate
- ❏ Patient
- ❏ Persistent
- ❏ Persuasive
- ❏ Problem solver

- ❏ Producer of events and materials
- ❏ Public speaker
- ❏ Questioner
- ❏ Recognizer of the impact of systems
- ❏ Reflective
- ❏ Resilient
- ❏ Respectful
- ❏ Responsible
- ❏ Self-confident
- ❏ Singer
- ❏ Sensitive
- ❏ Storyteller
- ❏ Supportive
- ❏ Trustworthy
- ❏ Video creator
- ❏ Visioner of change
- ❏ Willing to learn more
- ❏ Willing to share personal stories
- ❏ Writer of letters, articles, books, blogs, songs, plays and so on

What skills do you have that are not on this list?

. . . .

. . . .

. . . .

Review the items you checked on the skills list. While you will likely bring all of your skills to any project you undertake, circle the top three skills you could incorporate into your project to make a difference.

I care! Social justice topics interests checklist

The following alphabetical list includes a variety of social issues.[3] There are many more issues to consider. Please write in topics which you care about that are not on this list.

Place a star/asterisk (*) in the box for anything that is a top priority for you. Place a plus sign (+) in the box for anything that you care about. Use a minus sign (–) or leave blank the boxes for items that are not an immediate concern for you.

- ❏ Animals: supporting all life on Earth

- ❏ Black power: healing, promoting joy and an end to anti-Black racism (see also racial justice)

- ❏ Creating "a radical self-love economy" and "divesting from the Body-Shame Profit Complex,"[4] as Sonia Renee Taylor says

- ❏ Democracy and representative leadership, voting rights, ending voter suppression

- ❏ Disability justice: ensuring accessibility, adaptive technology, full inclusion and acceptance; ending social stigma, violence and discrimination

❏ Economic justice: increasing the minimum wage to a living wage; ending the wage gap/opportunity gap; ensuring equitable distribution of wealth and access to resources for all; providing a universal basic income

❏ Education justice: ensuring equity and full funding; requiring teaching of thorough and accurate history and cultural humility courses

❏ Elder issues: healthcare, housing, connection

❏ Ending mass incarceration and the Prison Industrial Complex: creating community security and transformative justice; ending militarization of the police

❏ Environmental justice: ending policies and practices causing global warming and harm to the Earth; creating sustainable practices for the Earth, growing food in communities and individually; returning land to the care of Indigenous stewards; making reparations for communities most impacted by pollution/toxic/hazardous waste

❏ Funding and empowering under-resourced (underinvested, underserved) communities with housing, jobs, education, healthcare/mental/behavioral health and wellness initiatives, art and cultural initiatives

❏ Gender justice: ending violence against women, girls, femmes, trans and non-binary people; ending patriarchy and the gender binary (see also transgender justice); creating a consent culture; ending the gendered wage gap; establishing equal pay for equal work

❏ Healing: creating/supporting spaces for individuals and communities to share practices that promote health and well being in body, mind and spirit

❏ Healthcare: supporting universal, free "Medicare for All" healthcare with no restrictions

❏   Housing security: housing unhoused people and communities (including people displaced by gentrification)

❏   Human trafficking: ending exploitation and profiteering of forced labor

❏   Poverty, food insecurity/hunger, housing insecurity: ending the injustices which perpetuate these inequities; funding social services and policies which ensure that every person has their basic needs met

❏   Immigrant justice: ending deportation, separation of families and incarceration of undocumented people; accepting and welcoming refugees and asylum seekers

❏   Indigenous sovereignty: returning land and resources to Indigenous tribes/nations; paying reparations; honoring and following the leadership and directives of environmental stewards (land, water and air protectors); restoring cultural practices, languages, place names and traditional tribal ways; cultivating healing spaces; divesting from colonial power; bringing awareness and action to the Missing and Murdered Indigenous Womxn, Girls, and Two Spirits program

❏   Intersectionality: using an analysis of power which considers the complex ways oppressions compound the harm caused to people of multiple marginalized identities

❏   Legislation: ending corporate influence in the legislative process

❏   Lesbian gay bisexual (queer) justice: ensuring legal protection in education, employment, housing and healthcare; ending "conversion therapy", violence and discrimination; fostering acceptance and ending social stigma

❏   Mental/behavioral health services and support: funding all care needs, including recovery/addiction services, and suicide prevention; fostering acceptance and ending social stigma

- ❏ Mutual aid: connecting with a community group to offer and receive resources and emotional support

- ❏ Preserving, growing and evolving cultural practices

- ❏ Racial justice: ending racialization and laws, policies and practices that harm BIPOC; dismantling white supremacy; paying reparations; funding healing, building power, self-determination and representation; resourcing historically underinvested communities; ensuring equity in all systems and institutions; providing cultural humility training for healthcare providers, educators and all service professionals

- ❏ Religious acceptance: ending Islamaphobia, anti-Semitism and all other intolerant policies and practices which target and harm people based on religion; promoting acceptance

- ❏ Reproductive rights: ensuring access to safe and affordable (and legal!) reproductive health services; ensuring full self-determination over one's body

- ❏ Sexual health education: ensuring medical accuracy and including all genders and sexualities, consent, pleasure, sexually transmitted infections and body dysmorphia

- ❏ Sex work: Legalizing sex work and ensuring labor/human rights. Ending stigma, violence and discrimination

- ❏ Transgender justice: ensuring legal protection in education, employment, housing and healthcare; ending violence, discrimination and gender identity "conversion therapy"; dismantling the gender binary; ending policies and practices identifying and separating people by gender; fostering acceptance and ending social stigma; providing non-binary and trans-affirming care training for healthcare providers, educators and all service professionals

- ❏ Unlearning and dismantling white supremacy: acknowledging privilege, history and harms; ending cultural appropriation; de-centering whiteness; respecting and valuing all cultures

❏   Women's rights (see Gender justice)

❏   Workers' rights: ensuring safe working conditions, benefits, rights to organize/collective bargaining (see Economic justice)

❏   Young people's power: honoring the wisdom; engaging with and following the leadership of people of all ages

Write in:

. . . .

. . . .

. . . .

Re-read your list. Put a circle around your top three social justice interests.

To which institution/system do you intend to direct your efforts?
Check all that apply (✓):

❏   Education/Schools   ❏   Media

❏   Employment/Jobs   ❏   Medical/Healthcare

❏   Government/Political   ❏   Military

❏   Housing   ❏   Prison industrial complex

❏   Legal   ❏   Religious

Write in:

. . . .

. . . .

. . . .

To what end?

Check all that apply (✓):

- ❏   Challenge unjust laws and policies

- ❏   Challenge unjust practices

- ❏   Challenge social norms of the dominant culture

- ❏   Challenge the lack of representation

- ❏   Challenge harm to the planet

- ❏   Push for inclusive and equitable laws

- ❏   Push for inclusive and equitable policies and practices

- ❏   Push for reparations

- ❏   Create new media (increase representation)

- ❏   Implement new community safety models

- ❏   Build and serve community

- ❏   Create healing spaces

- ❏   Create environmental sustainability practices

Write in:

....

....

....

Through what process?

❑ Art   ❑ Legal challenges

❑ Community organizing   ❑ Legislation/lobbying

❑ Education   ❑ Policy development

Write in:

....

....

....

Which of these actions are you motivated to take?

Check as many as apply (✓):

❑ Attend a demonstration/protest/rally

❑ Attend and speak up at a school board, city council or political meeting

❑ Build coalitions

❑ Conduct a survey (school climate, neighborhood/community concerns, what friends and family want to learn)

❑ Contact (call and/or write to) political representatives to express concern or support

❑ Create an event/project/conference to uplift my community; organize actions and events for empowerment and transformation (walk-a-thon, Rainbow Dance, teach-in, etc.)

❑ Create an info graphic

❑ Create art for empowerment

- ❏ Create publicity

- ❏ Donate money/time/resources

- ❏ Educate others

- ❏ Hold a conference

- ❏ Hold a silent auction

- ❏ Hold space for healing

- ❏ Host a poetry slam, dance, fashion event, music or performance event

- ❏ Host a speaker

- ❏ Learn about and practice my culture (ask elders!)

- ❏ Learn about the history of the land on which you live and the experiences of Indigenous peoples and people who were enslaved in that region; honor their lives, support their current efforts

- ❏ Listen to, support and empower people with marginalized identities

- ❏ Meet with elected political leaders to express concerns or an interest in partnership

- ❏ Meet with leaders of local companies to express concerns or an interest in partnership

- ❏ Organize or help organize a demonstration/protest/rally

- ❏ Produce a play

- ❏ Produce a web series

- ❏ Run for political office

- ❏ Start a social media campaign

- ❏ Start a fundraiser

- ❏ Support BIPOC businesses
- ❏ Vote, help with voter registration, volunteer at polling sites to ensure fair elections
- ❏ Write a book

Write in:

....

....

....

Review the items you selected. Circle the top three actions you are motivated to take.

Through which of your strengths/interests?

Check all that apply (✓):

- ❏ Acting
- ❏ Animal care
- ❏ App creation
- ❏ Campaigning
- ❏ Camping
- ❏ Child care
- ❏ Cleaning
- ❏ Coloring
- ❏ Collage

- ❏ Communication/ Language
- ❏ Cooking/Baking
- ❏ Cosmetology/ Beauty
- ❏ Dance/ Movement
- ❏ Drawing/ Illustrating
- ❏ Event hosting
- ❏ Fashion/Clothing design

- ❏ Film-making
- ❏ Furniture making
- ❏ Gardening
- ❏ Genealogy
- ❏ Graphic design
- ❏ Healing
- ❏ Hospitality
- ❏ Interior design
- ❏ Journalism

- ❏ Listening
- ❏ Knitting/ Crocheting
- ❏ Magic
- ❏ Meteorology
- ❏ Mindfulness/ Meditation
- ❏ Murals (designing, creating)
- ❏ Music (playing, songwriting)
- ❏ Painting
- ❏ Performance art
- ❏ Photography

- ❏ Playwriting
- ❏ Podcasting
- ❏ Poetry (writing/ performing/ spoken word)
- ❏ Public speaking
- ❏ Quilt making
- ❏ Rapping
- ❏ Reading
- ❏ Researching
- ❏ Sculpting
- ❏ Singing
- ❏ Skating/ skateboarding

- ❏ Sports
- ❏ Storytelling
- ❏ Teaching
- ❏ Tech/Information systems/support
- ❏ Theater (costume crew, tech crew, makeup crew)
- ❏ Tutoring
- ❏ Walking
- ❏ Web design
- ❏ Writing

Write in:

....

....

....

Review the items you selected. Circle the top three interests/strengths you want to use.

My project to make a difference: Putting it all together!

Look back over the checklists in this chapter. Transfer your top selections for each of these categories:

Re-write your top three social justice **commitments** (from the beginning of the chapter):

1. ....

2. ....

3. ....

Write your top three **skills** that you can use to make a difference:

1. ....

2. ....

3. ....

Write your top three "I care!" social justice **topic interests**:

1. ....

2. ....

3. ....

Write the institution/system you intend to **direct your efforts towards**:

....

Write your goal(s) from the **"To what end?"** list:

....

Record your thoughts from the **"Through what process?"** list:

. . . .

Write your top three items from the **"Which of these actions are you motivated to take?"** list:

1. . . . .

2. . . . .

3. . . . .

Write your top three items from the **"Through which of your strengths/ interests?"** list:

1. . . . .

2. . . . .

3. . . . .

Take some time to reflect on everything you recorded for each category. Give yourself space to allow your project ideas to gel. Use this space to write what you notice as you bring it all together. Do you feel an energy building and an intention to create? Do you feel unsure of how to proceed? Do you need more time and space to gather your thoughts? All of that is just fine! Trust that everything is unfolding in a way that makes your project possible. Pause, breathe and feel into your body and energy and sense whatever is happening. Write about your project ideas or your feelings/sensations or draw or dance or sing or express yourself in your unique way, or connect with a friend. Use this space to reflect on and dream about your project. We'll keep thinking through more details in the next section.

Journaling about my project

....

....

....

....

....

....

....

....

....

....

....

....

....

....

....

Drawing about my project

Keep thinking it through!

Let's consider more details about the project. It's always a great idea to brainstorm and allow yourself to dream big! Answer any or all of these questions or write your own questions and address them!

Who?

Who is centered in this project/event? Who is the audience you hope to attract? Who can you share your ideas with? Who can you get feedback from to ensure you are considering cultural sensitivity? Who will benefit from the project/event? Who needs to know about it? Who else is involved? Who will you collaborate with? Who needs to give permission/consent for use of space for an event? Who are the space holders for the project/event? Who are the volunteers or paid personnel?

. . . .

. . . .

. . . .

What?

What is the intention of this project/event? What do you hope to accomplish? What do you want to happen before, during and after the project/event? What will the project/event look like, sound like, feel like? What accessibility items will be considered and included? What measures of effectiveness will you use? (Will you seek feedback from participants on the planning committee and others?) What if the project/event/work is already being done by others? What could you do to support existing efforts?

. . . .

. . . .

. . . .

When?

When will the project/event happen? When is the best time to start? Will there be an end date? A project may be a short-term event, a longer-term venture or a lifelong commitment. When will you assess your progress? When will you meet with collaborators? When will you evaluate the outcome (if there is an outcome)?

....

....

....

Where?

Where will the project/event take place? Where will you advertise the project/event?

....

....

....

Why?

Why are you taking this action? (Consider: why *you* are taking this action; why you are taking *this* action.)

....

....

....

How?

How will group agreements be created and upheld? How will you communicate with collaborators? How will conflicts be addressed? How will you communicate accessibility offerings to potential participants? How will you know if the project/event met the intentions? How will you practice self-care during the process of organizing/creating your project/ event? How will you celebrate your accomplishment(s) along the way or on completion? How much will the event/project cost? Is there a budget? How will funds be raised/secured/donated? How will the recipient(s) of the donation be decided? How will you keep the momentum going?

. . . .

. . . .

. . . .

What if your school/district or community is not supportive of the project that you want to offer? What would it look like to proceed without that support? You can do it! Decide on a designated time and place for a meet-up and just start talking to a group of interested people. That could be online, at a coffee shop, a library or a park. Chanice Lee, teen activist, author, speaker and creator of The Melanin Diary blog, writes about her extensive research on students' rights at school, home, work, with the police and in court in her book *Young Revolutionary: A Teen's Guide to Activism*,[5] which also features stories of teen activists. Remember, your voice matters!

The STARS are aligned!

What do you need to get your project started or sustain the momentum? STARS!

Space   **R**esources

Time   **S**upport

Allies/Accomplices

Remember that you are limitless and that your creative potential is amazing! Let's channel that energy!

Jot down your thoughts for each category of STARS for your primary project.

Space: What space do you need? That might be a physical location, mental/emotional space or an online platform. How can you access that space?

. . . .

. . . .

. . . .

Time: What time do you need? Is your schedule full? Is there something that is consuming your time (social media, binge watching TV?) that could be put aside or minimized in order to make time for your action project? What time will you set aside to devote to your project?

. . . .

. . . .

. . . .

Allies/Accomplices: Who do you need to collaborate with you on this project? Friends, family, classmates, co-workers, neighbors, community members, social media network, who else? How will you engage potential collaborators? What ally action will they be taking?

. . . .

. . . .

. . . .

Resources: What supplies and equipment are necessary to bring your project to realization? What resources are you creating that will be sustained through the momentum you are generating?

....

....

....

Support: What support do you need to make this project happen? Think about financial support, emotional support, physical support and more. Are there grants available for your project? Could you start a funding campaign online? Do you need a friend to be an accountability buddy or cheerleader to remind you of your power and keep you on track? What nutrition/hydration, exercise and sleep do you need to keep you feeling your best through this project? What affirmations can you say to remind yourself of your power and purpose?

....

....

....

What project are you feeling most passionate about at this moment? It is absolutely essential that we prioritize self-care. If you feel drained or overly stressed, please make today's priority a self-care project! Restoration, healing and recovery are ongoing and critical components for longevity and sustaining the momentum of making a difference for social justice. How can we give and serve from a place of empowerment? Sometimes it's easier to care for other people than it is to look at ourselves or care for ourselves. If that is the case, start by noticing how you feel. As often as you can, bring your awareness to your body and heart. What feels nourishing and empowering? What feels depleting and disempowering?

Can we find ways to move through challenging situations to draw strength from those who have gone before us? Notice your courage. Honor your power and resilience. See the beauty in yourself, others and nature. Look with love at your efforts to make the world a better place.

Words of advice

Let's enjoy hearing some words of **advice** to people who want to make a difference from Alise, Grayson, Helen and Soul.

Alise

Be kind with yourself. If you are just going into something, take it slowly. Sometimes when I jump in and try to dedicate all my time to a lot of things, it's exhausting and I don't get anything done. So, it's okay to put yourself first and to really go along the journey. Sometimes people see activism as trying to delve into every single thing. I think it's much more meaningful when you find something that you're really, truly passionate about and try to make change in it rather than go from one cause to the next and the next. Really focus your efforts and focus on one task. Get it done, move on to the next and try not to spread yourself too thin.

Lastly, advice that I give to anyone is diversify your crew. I see so many people doing activism and then they go back to their friends and all their friends are white or all their friends are straight and they're not really learning anything besides what they read. So, it's super important: the basis of activism is empathy and love and compassion.

Grayson

First and foremost, you always can make a difference. The first step is believing in yourself, knowing that your voice is worthy of being echoed and *you* have to take that first step. You might be surprised at how much you can get done by reaching out to people. If you want to go and speak at that school or hospital, reach out to them.

If you want to get in contact with another transgender activist or whatever activist it might be, then contact them. People who are passionate about their cause will most likely be willing to help you and talk to you. Connect with those people and create a community, create an organization, create a platform to share your message, to share your education. Once you start building that, then it only goes up from there.

Helen

Whatever you are creating and interested in creating, keep doing that. Whatever the people around you think about it or whatever backlash you're facing, what you're making is worthwhile, so keep working on it. If it's art, if it's activism, if it's whatever—keep making it. And also build a support network. Find a place and people you can go to where you feel safe and cherished and supported. Those have been the things that have been the most
useful for me, in my own experience—continuing to make the stuff that I've made, and knowing that there was somewhere I could turn when I was not feeling good at all, where people would love me and support me and have my best interests at heart. I know that not everyone has the ability to go somewhere and get out of the situations they're in, but if there is a way that you can do that somewhat or someone you can call, or somewhere you feel safe that you can go to, try to cultivate that.

It's important to remember that you're not going to change someone's mind in a day. There may be people who are annoyed by thinking about social justice, about conversations about sexism and racism, and say, "Aren't we over this?" or, "Why are you trying to do this?" or, "Oh, come on, you're taking it too far." So, if someone says something hurtful that makes you feel not respected and not taken seriously, say, "Hey, that was not acceptable. I'm not okay with this," and set a hard boundary. Sometimes it means walking away and letting someone else who isn't being attacked or doesn't have identities that are as vulnerable handle it. Address the feelings later once you're in a safe environment. It's just a sad thing that some people are cruel or try to use cruelty as a way to protect themselves from having to address difficult truths.

Soul

I can't really remember how I got started, but just do it, start with yourself. Look to yourself and know that you are not free from the bigotry that exists in society and you need to learn more. We're all racist. I've seen people out there who are like, "I'm not classist." Look out for that in yourself. Start with your family if you're able to have these discussions with them. You can find groups around you, like I found Diversity Trainers. There's also Food Not Bombs. There are other groups doing the work, democratic parties. There's a communist group that runs English as a second language classes and teaches people about their rights as tenants, hooking them up with lawyers who are part of non-profit groups and are able to take on cases. Just directly, do the work.

Reflection: What's already happening?

Remember, you don't have to reinvent the wheel or go it alone! Where can you look (online) for people, organizations and communities that are already out there doing the work in the service of humanity and the planet? Can you join forces with them?

. . . .

. . . .

. . . .

From seed to fruit

Let's think about your project in the stages of growing. This can be a visualization or an art project. Use your creativity!

Imagine a fruit tree. Here are some examples of fruit that grows on trees:

Apples	Grapefruit	Oranges
Apricots	Lemons	Peaches
Avocados	Mangoes	Pears
Cherries	Nectarines	Plums
Figs	Olives	Pomegranates

Which fruit most appeals to you right now? Pick your favorite! Imagine that fruit in detail. What is the color? What is the texture of the outside and inside? What do the seeds, stone or pit look like? Do you have an image in mind of the tree that grows that fruit? How do the flowers look? Do they have a fragrance? What is the scent of the ripe fruit? How does it taste? Does it make your mouth water? Hold on to that feeling.

Sketch a drawing of your fruit, its tree with roots or perhaps its seed(s)/pit/stone. Are there words that come to mind? Write them on your drawing of the roots, trunk, branches, and fruit. What are the nutrients that are needed to sustain this tree? Perhaps write those words on the ground and sky in your drawing. If you prefer, you can use the illustration that appears after the draw-in box.

. . . .

. . . .

. . . .

. . . .

Seed spiral tree

Now think about your social justice project. Give it a title. Write that title at the top of the fruit/tree drawing or in the spiral. What elements are needed to create and sustain the life of this project? Write those on the drawing as well.

Now, imagine all of the STARS align and your project is complete. It is reality! For now, just set aside whatever obstacles you might expect to encounter. Truly allow yourself to bask in the glow of your completed project. Know that IT IS DONE! How does it feel in your body when you think about it? What sensations are there? What other elements are there? Write a few notes on how you feel:

. . . .

. . . .

. . . .

The word fruition literally means bearing fruit. We hold the vision of our ideas for social justice coming to fruition. You are planting seeds which will germinate, take root, grow strong and bear fruit. May your efforts create space for liberation to flourish! Your actions will certainly make a difference in your own life. Even if you do not get to see or taste the fruits of your labor, trust that others will in time.

Taking steps

What are the steps to bringing your project to life? Write a few thoughts here. Feel free to number them if they need to happen in sequence.

. . . .

. . . .

. . . .

Keeping motivated!

Are you encouraged by recording your actions and acknowledging your efforts? If so, use this chart or your journal to track your progress. Give yourself a smiley face or a star for your actions if that feels fun and motivational to you!

Date	☆	Action	Notes/Reflections

Please use the prompts and checklists in this chapter again and again. Once one project is complete, take time to review your responses or start fresh and create a new set of responses. The possibilities are infinite! Your energy and creativity are so needed and valued. Challenging the systems and structures of society that create unjust policies, practices and thinking is a lifelong process. As Ibram X. Kendi reminds us, "being an antiracist requires persistent self-awareness...and regular self-examination."[6] Devoting your energies towards justice and equity is a beautiful lifelong practice.

Thank you for spending this time growing and learning in your service to transformation and liberation. It is an honor to be on this journey with you. When we use our life force energies in service to humanity (and humanity includes you!), the inhabitants of the Earth and the Earth itself, we are transformed. That helps others around us to see what is possible. Keep living your visions for the greatest and highest good of all. Keep making a difference!

ENDNOTES

Introduction

1   Bodies as Resistance: Claiming the political act of being oneself. Sonya Renee Taylor. TEDxMarin. YouTube, uploaded by TEDx Talks, 18 October 2017, www.youtube.com/watch?v=MWI9AZkuPVg.

Chapter 1

1   Boom, K. (2015, August 4) *4 Tired Tropes That Perfectly Explain What Misogynoir Is – And How You Can Stop It.* Everyday Feminism. Retrieved January 30, 2021, from https://everydayfeminism.com/2015/08/4-tired-tropes-misogynoir.

2   Wulfhorst, E. (2020, June 5) *Creator of term "misogynoir" sees power in #hashtag activism.* Thomson Reuters Foundation. Retrieved January 30, 2021, from https://news.trust.org/item/20200605100134-aozhh.

3   Menakem, R. (2017) *My Grandmother's Hands: Racialized Trauma and the Pathway to Mending our Hearts and Bodies* (p.68). Las Vegas, NV: Central Recovery Press. For information on Somatic Abolitionism, see www.resmaa.com/movement (accessed January 30, 2021).

4   Lorde, A. (1984) *Sister Outsider: Essays and Speeches* (p.138). Berkeley, CA: The Crossing Press.

5   Dr. Howard Gardner conceived of the theory of Multiple Intelligences to expand and challenge understandings of intelligence beyond I.Q. tests. See more at: www.multipleintelligencesoasis.org/the-components-of-mi (accessed January 30, 2021).

6   Kendi, I. (2019) *How to Be an Antiracist* (p.8). New York, NY: One World.

7   Taylor, S. R. (2018) *The Body is Not an Apology: The Power of Radical Self-Love* (p.39). Oakland, CA: Berrett-Koehler Publishers.

8   Mingus, M. (2015, February 6) The Medical Industrial Complex. Retrieved January 30, 2021, from https://leavingevidence.files.wordpress.com/2015/02/mic-visual-version-2015-12.pdf.

9   Taylor, S. R. (2018) *The Body is Not an Apology: The Power of Radical Self-Love* (p.4). Oakland, CA: Berrett-Koehler Publishers. For more on "radical self-love for everybody and every body," see https://thebodyisnotanapology.com (accessed January 30, 2021).

10   Knowles, S., Gallagher, B., and McEwen, P. (2018) *My Anxiety Handbook: Getting Back on Track* (p.64). London: Jessica Kingsley Publishers.

11   Shea Maultsby (2021) www.peacefulpraise.com (accessed January 30, 2021).

12   "Mona Haydar—Good Body." YouTube, uploaded by mona haydar, January 13, 2020, www.youtube.com/watch?v=2SM39XoBVgw.

Chapter 2

1   Everbach, H. and Cooke, S. (2014) Recognizing Language that Dehumanizes People.

2   Kosciw, J., Clark, C., Truong, N. and Zongrone, A. (2020) *The 2019 National School Climate Survey: The Experiences of Lesbian, Gay, Bisexual, Transgender, and Queer Youth in Our Nation's Schools.* New York, NY: GLSEN. Retrieved January 30, 2021, from www.glsen.org/sites/default/files/2020-11/NSCS19-111820.pdf.

3   The Trevor Project. (2020) *2020 National Survey on LGBTQ Youth Mental Health.* New York, NY: The Trevor Project. Retrieved January 30, 2021, from www.thetrevorproject.org/survey-2020.

4   United Nations (1948) *Universal Declaration of Human Rights.* Retrieved January 30, 2021, from www.un.org/en/universal-declaration-human-rights.

5   Everbach, H. and Cooke, S. (2014) Recognizing Language that Dehumanizes People (p.1).

6   Lewis, V. (n.d) *Welcome to Reclaim UGLY.* Retrieved November 18, 2020, from https://reclaimugly.org.

7   Lewis, V. (n.d) *Mission & Values.* Retrieved November 18, 2020, from https://reclaimugly.org/about-us.

8   This activity was conceived of in a collaborative conversation with Kyomi Gregory-Martin, Ph.D., on March 7, 2020.

9   Menakem, R. (2017) *My Grandmother's Hands: Racialized Trauma and the Pathway to Mending our Hearts and Bodies.* Las Vegas, NV: Central Recovery Press.

10   This exercise was inspired by Resmaa Menakem's "Body Practice." Menakem, R. (2017) *My Grandmother's Hands: Racialized Trauma and the Pathway to Mending our Hearts and Bodies* (pp.31–32). Las Vegas, NV: Central Recovery Press.

Chapter 3

1   The Trevor Project. (2020) *2020 National Survey on LGBTQ Youth Mental Health.* New York, NY: The Trevor Project. Retrieved January 30, 2021, from www.thetrevorproject.org/survey-2020.

2   Shapiro, R. (2013) *Ethics of the Sages: Pirke Avot* (2:16). Woodstock, VT: SkyLight Paths.

3   Sarsour, L. (2020) *We Are Not Here to Be Bystanders: A Memoir of Love and Resistance* (p.227). New York, NY: 37 Ink.

4   Kimmerer, R. (2013) *Braiding Sweetgrass: Indigenous Wisdom, Scientific Knowledge and the Teachings of Plants* (p. 107). Minneapolis, MN: Milkweed Editions.

5   Kendi, I. (2019) *How to Be an Antiracist* (p.105). New York, NY: One World.

6   Eberhardt, J. (2020) *Biased: Uncovering the Hidden Prejudice that Shapes What We See, Think and Do* (p.170). New York, NY: Penguin Books.

Chapter 4

1   Based on Ralph Waldo Emerson's poem "To Laugh Often and Much."

2   Jonsson, M. (2013) *M-Joy Practically Speaking: Matrix Energetics and Living Your Infinite Potential* (p.186). California: M-Joy of Being.

Chapter 5

1   The Trevor Project. (2020) *2020 National Survey on LGBTQ Youth Mental Health*. New York, NY: The Trevor Project. Retrieved January 30, 2021, from www. thetrevorproject.org/survey-2020; and Kosciw, J., Clark, C., Truong, N. and Zongrone, A. (2020) *The 2019 National School Climate Survey: The Experiences of Lesbian, Gay, Bisexual, Transgender, and Queer Youth in Our Nation's Schools*. New York, NY: GLSEN. Retrieved January 30, 2021, from www.glsen.org/sites/default/files/2020-11/ NSCS19-111820.pdf.

2   James, S. E., Herman, J. L., Rankin, S., Keisling, M., Mottet, L. and Anafi, M. (2016) *Executive Summary of the Report of the 2015 U.S. Transgender Survey*. Washington, DC: National Center for Transgender Equality (p.2). Retrieved January 30, 2021, from https://transequality.org/sites/default/files/docs/usts/USTS-Executive-Summary-Dec17.pdf.

3   These questions are inspired by an activity Helen created for Diversity Trainers called "The Neutral Story." Everbach, H. (2015) The Neutral Story.

4   "Creating Self Portrait (2019) an Installation of Glass Flowers." YouTube, uploaded by Soul C Studios, June 11, 2020, www.youtube.com/watch?v=SYJjRs1EQ2w.

5   Schneider, P. and Paris, S. (2020) *Being a Super Trans Ally! A Creative Workbook and Journal for Young People*. London: Jessica Kingsley Publishers.

Chapter 6

1   Brach, T. (2003) *Radical Acceptance: Awakening the Love That Heals Fear and Shame*. New York, NY: Bantam Books.

2   Knowles, S., Gallagher, B. and McEwen, P. (2018) *My Anxiety Handbook: Getting Back on Track* (p.87). London: Jessica Kingsley Publishers.

Chapter 7

1   Learn more about the Colored Girls Museum: http://thecoloredgirlsmuseum.com (accessed January 28, 2021).

2   Freyd, J. J. (2020) What is DARVO? Retrieved January 30, 2021, from http://pages. uoregon.edu/dynamic/jjf/defineDARVO.html.

3   400 Years of Inequality. (n.d.) Retrieved January 30, 2021, from www.400yearsofinequality.org. See also www.drangelacosta.com.

Chapter 8

1   Mingus, M. for the Bay Area Transformative Justice Collective. (2016, June) Pods and Pod Mapping Worksheet. Retrieved January 30, 2021, from https://batjc. wordpress.com/pods-and-pod-mapping-worksheet.

2   Mingus, M. (2018) Transformative Justice: a brief description. Retrieved January 30, 2021, from https://transformharm.org/transformative-justice-a-brief-description.

3   Mia Mingus offers a framework for taking accountability through an apology. Mingus, M. (2019, December 18) How to give a genuine apology part 2: the apology – the what and the how. Retrieved January 30, 2021, from https://leavingevidence. wordpress.com/2019/12/18/how-to-give-a-good-apology-part-2-the-apology-the-what-and-the-how.

Chapter 9

1   Everbach, H. (2015) Rules of the Game.

2   DiAngelo, R. (2018) *White Fragility: Why It's So Hard for White People to Talk About Racism* (p.109, p.119). Boston, MA: Beacon Press.

3   DiAngelo, R. (2018) *White Fragility: Why It's So Hard for White People to Talk About Racism* (p.112). Boston, MA: Beacon Press.

4   Saad, L. (2020) *Me and White Supremacy: Combat Racism, Change the World, and Become a Good Ancestor*. Chicago, IL: Sourcebooks.

5   H.Res. 194 (110th): Apologizing for the enslavement and racial segregation of African-Americans. (2008, July 29). Retrieved January 30, 2021, from www.govtrack. us/congress/bills/110/hres194/text.

6   Electoral Justice Project of The Movement for Black Lives (2020). The BREATHE Act. Retrieved January 30, 2021, from https://breatheact.org.

7   Thompson, C. (2020, November 25) Returning the Land: Four Indigenous leaders share insights about the growing landback movement and what it means for the planet. *Grist*. Retrieved January 30, 2021, from https://grist.org/fix/indigenous-landback-movement-can-it-help-climate.

8   United Nations (2007, 13 September) *Declaration on the Rights of Indigenous Peoples*. Retrieved January 30, 2021, from www.un.org/development/desa/indigenouspeoples/wp-content/uploads/sites/19/2018/11/UNDRIP_E_web.pdf.

9   Thompson, C. (2020, November 25) Returning the Land: Four Indigenous leaders share insights about the growing landback movement and what it means for the planet. *Grist*. Retrieved January 30, 2021, from https://grist.org/fix/indigenous-landback-movement-can-it-help-climate.

Chapter 10

1   The Autistic Self Advocacy Network offers accessibility materials online. Autistic Self Advocacy Network. (n.d.) Accessibility Resources. Retrieved January 30, 2021, from https://autisticadvocacy.org/resources/accessibility. You can download disability access symbols from the Graphic Artists Guild: Graphic Artists Guild (n.d.) Downloadable Disability Access Symbols. Retrieved January 30, 2021, from https://graphicartistsguild.org/downloadable-disability-access-symbols.

2   U.S. Department of Justice, Civil Rights Division (n.d.) Americans with Disabilities Act. Retrieved January 30, 2021, from www.ada.gov.

3   Inspired by and parts are adapted from The Leeway Foundation's (2020) Art and Change Grant Guidelines "Social Change Intent/Vision" (p.5). Retrieved January 30, 2021, from www.leeway.org/images/blog/2020_ACG_Application_Guidelines_FINAL.pdf.

4   Taylor, S. R. (2018) *The Body is Not an Apology: The Power of Radical Self-Love* (p.43). Oakland, CA: Berrett-Koehler Publishers.

5   Lee, C. (2018) *Young Revolutionary: A Teen's Guide to Activism*. Atlanta, GA: YBF Publishing.

6   Kendi, I. (2019) *How to be an Antiracist* (p.23). New York, NY: One World.

ABOUT THE AUTHOR

Sherry Paris (she/her/hers) is a gay/queer white woman who lives on Lenape land (in Philadelphia) with her beloved life partner Mel. She is an author, illustrator and Diversity Trainer who was named as the National Liberty Museum's first "Teacher as Superhero" in 2017. Sherry is on a mission to co-create a world in which everyone is respected, included, accepted and appreciated for who they truly are and are resourced to thrive. She combines a passion for social justice with her love of education to design, write and lead interactive sensitivity trainings. Ms. Paris (her teacher name!) proudly collaborated with young people for 20 years to create a culture of belonging, acceptance and social consciousness through her leadership of a high school-based Diversity Training program. She holds a master's degree in the Science of Instruction from Drexel University and taught high school mathematics for 22 years. Sherry is the co-author and illustrator of the book *Being a Super Trans Ally! A Creative Workbook and Journal for Young People*.